PCI DSS: A PRACTICAL GUIDE TO IMPLEMENTING AND MAINTAINING COMPLIANCE

THIRD EDITION

PCI DSS: A Practical Guide to Implementing and Maintaining Compliance

THIRD EDITION

STEVE WRIGHT

IT Governance Publishing

Every possible effort has been made to ensure that the information contained in this book is accurate at the time of going to press, and the publisher and the author cannot accept responsibility for any errors or omissions, however caused. No responsibility for loss or damage occasioned to any person acting, or refraining from action, as a result of the material in this publication can be accepted by the publisher or the author.

Apart from any fair dealing for the purposes of research or private study, or criticism or review, as permitted under the Copyright, Designs and Patents Act 1988, this publication may only be reproduced, stored or transmitted, in any form, or by any means, with the prior permission in writing of the publisher or, in the case of reprographic reproduction, in accordance with the terms of licences issued by the Copyright Licensing Agency. Enquiries concerning reproduction outside those terms should be sent to the publisher at the following address:

IT Governance Publishing
IT Governance Limited
Unit 3, Clive Court
Bartholomew's Walk
Cambridgeshire Business Park
Ely
Cambridgeshire
CB7 4EH
United Kingdom

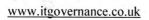

www.itgovernance.co.uk

The author has asserted the rights of the author under the Copyright, Designs and Patents Act, 1988, to be identified as the author of this work.

First published in the United Kingdom in 2008
by IT Governance Publishing (ISBN 978-1-905356-45-4).

Second edition 2009 (ISBN 978-1-84928-023-5).
Third edition 2011 (ISBN 978-1-84929-186-7).

FOREWORD

The objective of this (revised 2011) practical guide is to give entities practical advice and tips on the entire Payment Card Industry (PCI) implementation process. It provides a roadmap, helping entities to navigate the broad and sometimes confusing Payment Card Industry Data Security Standard (PCI DSS) v2 and shows them how to build and maintain a sustainable PCI compliance programme.

This latest revision also includes increased guidance on how to ensure your compliance programme is 'sustainable' (see *Chapter 9*). This has been based on real-life scenarios and should help to ensure your PCI compliance programme remains compliant.

Although the guide starts with sections on why and what is PCI, it is not intended to replace the 'publicly available' PCI information. Thus, it is designed more to provide additional and practical guidance to help support IT directors, project managers, executives and IT security officers who have been tasked with ensuring PCI compliance within their entity.

So, this book looks to serve those who have been given the responsibility of PCI; it does not attempt to provide all the answers. It should be read, absorbed and digested, only with a good helping of other good PCI 'publicly available' information. (Please refer to *www.pcisecuritystandards.org* for more information.) In other words – it will help an entity get started and, hopefully furnish the reader with enough of the fundamental basics to create, design and build a comprehensive PCI compliance framework that maintains and demonstrates compliance well into the future.

PREFACE

Looking towards the future, on average, 77% of entities are anticipating an increase in online revenues during 2011. For 2011, nearly four out of five merchants that are forecasting growth expect to see increases in e-commerce revenue of up to 40%.

So, for many entities' chief financial officers, chief information officers, chief technology officers, and chief security officers, this presents three challenges, it will;

1 Increase online revenues causing the logistics, call-centres, order fulfilment, etc, etc. to further 'creak' at the seams.
2 Increase the dependency on the already overburdened IT department. Thus creating the need to 'change' the IT organisation from a traditional IT department to a more IT marketing focused or e-commerce support function.
3 Increase the IT security compliance burden; therefore, increasing the need for the growth and maintenance of core compliance (or auditing) skills. The average size of IT compliance review teams has risen quite considerably from an average of six full time staff members in 2009 to ten in 2011.[1]

All of this comes at a time of unparalleled pressure on IT budgets, its people and, more specifically, the security people employed to protect cardholder data (ChD). Like us, we all thought the Payment Card Industry Data Security Standard (PCI DSS) was going to spell the end of the road

---

[1] UK Online Fraud Report 2011.

for criminals who were 'cashing in' on the supposedly easy target of credit card theft – and its subsequent fraudulent use of cardholder data. The theory being, it would be harder to obtain the cardholder data in the first place; due to the more robust and standardised approach to data and IT security (under the PCI DSS regime).

Unfortunately, as we have seen, and as countless surveys conclude, many entities are still struggling to demonstrate compliance, with costs spiralling out of control. Analysts Gartner estimate that Level 1 merchants (retailers who process over 6 million credit card transactions per year) on average spent $2.7m on compliance, with Level 2 merchants (retailers who process between 1 and 6 million credit card transactions per year) are spending $1.1m on average to remain compliant. They also state that Level 1 and 2 merchants have increased their spending fivefold over the last 18 months, with 8% of retailers being fined and 22% being threatened with fines.

Yet, despite the pressure of fines being imposed, entities continue to struggle with PCI DSS compliance, and worse still, some of these entities which have achieved PCI DSS compliance, are still suffering from costly and embarrassing data losses/breaches (for example, TJ MAXX, Hannaford Brothers). Gartner go on to recommend that these entities look at the possibility of further data segregation, or outsourcing to reduce the scope of compliance, but this doesn't take away the responsibility of PCI compliance, as this still lies at the door of the cardholder data collector and data owner

These findings are in themselves not very surprising, as anyone hoping PCI DSS was going to be the industry's 'silver bullet' to a systemic and ever-demanding data security challenge was unrealistic or slightly divorced from reality. PCI DSS is a good security baseline on which compliance can be set, achieved, measured and improved, but it will not provide all the answers, and will not necessarily change the thoughts that plague every CIO's mind – how can I provide adequate assurance that my cardholder data is appropriately protected and secured, given minimal resources and squeezed budgets?

In order to address this question, we first need to understand why there is a need for PCI DSS, and why it will become (if it is not already) a prerequisite for conducting business in the modern age of online consumers and tech savvy 'Generation Y' consumers[2] and, in particular, if we dare hope for a consumer-led recovery.

Firstly, there is sufficient evidence that consumers are changing the way they shop and we don't have to look far to appreciate the value of providing secure credit card transactions; for example, Cybersource 7th Annual 2011 UK Online Fraud Report[3], found that some 66% of those questioned were concerned about the safety of shopping on line.

Yet, despite these concerns, millions of consumers are continuing to use credit cards every day for online purchases. VISA Europe reported that its 360 million card holders collectively purchased goods online to the value of over £1.16 trillion in 2009[4]. To further exacerbate the

---

[2] Joanna Krotz – Small business marketing and management issues publisher.
[3] Seventh Annual UK Online Fraud Report, Jan 2011, CyberSource.
[4] Plunkett Research Limited, Guide to the Banking Industry, March 2009.

problem, we are faced with an ever-evolving and more demanding consumer (driven by Generation Y), with factors such as those listed below all contributing to an overall global demand in better security of cardholder data. These factors include:

- Banks seeing a huge growth in the demand for online services.
- Credit card issuers and debt holders facing a difficult market/consumer, as pressures to pay down debts and charge less for services become commonplace.
- Credit card technologies advancing with better security and contactless payment solutions.
- Managing bank accounts via mobile devices, and wireless (or contactless) payment systems increasing demand for more applications to support demand for these services.

All of these factors play a role in the need for greater cardholder data security and, therefore, the need for PCI DSS will remain and become ever more prevalent in the competitive world of consumerism.

The consumer space is not alone; governments from around the world are taking up arms in this space. In the UK, the UK Government published its first Cyber Security Strategy. It was a calling for more moves towards greater security surrounding the use of credit card data. In another paper entitled 'Digital Britain', the UK Government stated 'that by 2012 £1 in every £5 spend in the UK will be spent online and if that is going to be a reality, then significant more effort needs to be made towards gaining consumer trust', as, with the £50 billion of consumer purchases and sales through e-commerce that takes place online[5] now is the time to really start thinking about how your entity can look to further integrate PCI DSS compliance into 'Business as Usual'.

NOTE: Some good work has previously been carried out in this area: both ISO27001 and ISO27002 (formally BS7799) are intended to provide an international information 'security baseline' of 133 controls, in an attempt to standardise on security best practice and a standard approach to risk assessment. ISO27001 has gone a long way to help standardise on an approach to security policy, processes and procedures to help keep the bad guys out, and the good guys (or to keep 'sensitive' data) within our direct control.

This is all good stuff, but is it enough? In a recent online fraud survey, figures show that the fraud challenge has not decreased since the introduction of PCI, but has, in fact, increased. The report states 'that fraud losses now consume more than 1% of revenue for 37% of UK online merchants; 13% lose more than 5% of their revenue. In a tough economic climate, these losses could be the difference between success and failure for an online business'.

In addition, the breaches in late 2008 and early 2009 of RBS World Pay and Heartland Payment Systems, which compromised over an estimated 100 million cardholders, exemplify the irresistible attraction of major transaction processors (i.e. the banks). So, despite PCI DSS being applicable to those entities that store, transmit or process cardholder information payments, encompassing service

---

[5] UK Cyber Security Strategy June 2009.

providers, merchant acquirers, third party processors and even data storage entities, the danger of not knowing where your data is can prove fundamental to demonstrating and maintaining PCI compliance.

This all tends to paint a negative picture, but what more could be done? As it is well acknowledged that merchants and service providers are bearing the costs associated with securing our credit card or cardholder data, we need to understand (more now than ever) the true scope of where PCI DSS is applicable, and how we can assist the business in obtaining the true value delivered by PCI DSS.

In today's environment, security has become a consideration for every type of business and, by following the standardised, industry-wide procedures of PCI DSS, entities can achieve real value, including:

- Protection of their customers' personal data.
- Boost customer confidence through a higher level of data security.
- Insulate themselves from financial losses and remediation costs.
- Maintain customer trust, and safeguard the reputation of their brand.
- Provide a complete 'health check' for any business that stores or transmits customer information.

ABOUT THE AUTHOR

Steve Wright is an 'information security' subject matter expert in the area of strategy, security organisational design or 'transformation' and security risk and governance frameworks. With over 18 years of experience in design and implementation of security solutions, including the design and architecture of information security control frameworks. Steve helps C-suite executives and boards of the UK's FTSE 100 organisations ensure their security posture is appropriate and adequate to the appetite of the business. He has a practical 'hands-on', 'no nonsense approach to risk and security which allows him to cut to the chase and provide expert advice through collaboration and partnering with the business and IT department entity. He also founded the UK ISO27002 information security knowledge portal – *www.ISO27002.Info* – and can be contacted at PwC or on *steve.wright@ISO27002.info*.

ACKNOWLEDGEMENTS

I would especially like to thank my wife and children for putting up with me being locked away in my study for countless weekends and evenings.

There is a fantastic amount of really well-written and useful whitepapers on this subject and, therefore, I would like to thank all these people who have in some way helped to formulate this guide.

The PCI Security Standards Council (PCI SSC) website (*www.pcisecuritystandards.org*) contains a number of additional resources, including:

- Attestations of Compliance *Navigating PCI DSS: Understanding the Intent of the Requirements*
- The *PCI DSS and PA-DSS Glossary of Terms, Abbreviations and Acronyms*
- Frequently Asked Questions (FAQs)
- Information Supplements and Guidelines.

I strongly recommend you spend an appropriate amount of time to read and digest all the good information that is freely available at *www.pcisecuritystandards.org*.

I hope you find this practical guide useful, and welcome feedback on any of the processes and recommendations detailed within.

CONTENTS

Contents

Contents

BACKGROUND

What is PCI?

In 2001, VISA and MasterCard each instigated basic levels of credit card security compliance programs, in which both retailers (known as merchants), banks and entities that provided cardholder authentication and authorisation services (known as service providers) were required to demonstrate compliance.

Visa had created CISP (Cardholder Information Security Programme) and MasterCard had created SDP (Site Data Protection). And each security standard placed a heavy burden on both merchants and service providers; as they had to comply with several different programs. Fortunately, by 2004 VISA and MasterCard had set up a joint data security standard known as the Payment Card Industry (PCI) Data Security Standard (DSS), which incorporated both the CISP and SDP requirements, and ensured merchants and service providers had only one security standard in which to demonstrate compliance.

By 2006, the PCI DSS had further evolved and included input from other credit card providers (JCB International, AMEX and Discovery), this agreement culminated in the formulation of the PCI Security Standards Council (PCI SSC). This council was then given the responsibility for the development, management, education, and awareness of PCI DSS and other related standards.

Adherence to the Standard may require (depending upon the quantity of cardholder data being stored, transmitted, accessed), specific compliance certification by PCI SSC sanctioned Approved Scanning Vendors (ASVs), which provide periodic vulnerability scanning of Internet facing systems, as well as Qualified Security Assessors (QSAs), which validate adherence to the PCI DSS to provide confidence that cardholder information is adequately protected.

In addition to PCI DSS, the Security Standards Council defines the Payment Application – Data Security Standard (PA-DSS). This standard allows vendors, manufactures and entities which develop payment processing applications and physical PIN Entry Devices (PED), to adhere to a standardised device security requirement, this standard also incorporates how the device will be tested (methodology) and the approval processes for manufacturers of Personal Identification Number (PIN) devices.

The PCI Security Standards Council first released version 1.1 of the PCI Standard, and then updated the Standard to version 1.2 in October 2008. This was further updated to 1.2.1 in July 2009, and version 2 was released in October 2010. Since its inception, it has become the 'de-facto' security standard within the card industry for both merchant[6] and service provider.[7]

---

[6] **Merchant:** Business entity that is directly involved in the processing, storage, transmission, and switching of transaction data and cardholder information or both.

[7] **Service provider:** Business entity that is not a payment card brand member or a merchant directly involved in the processing, storage, transmission, and switching of transaction data and cardholder

The purpose of PCI DSS is to ensure that sensitive cardholder data is always secure and the Standard comprises six high-level objectives, broken down further into twelve individual (mandatory) requirements:

- **Build and maintain a secure network.**
  o Requirement 1: Install and maintain a firewall configuration to protect cardholder data.
  o Requirement 2: Do not use vendor-supplied defaults for system passwords and other security parameters.
- **Protect cardholder data.**
  o Requirement 3: Protect stored cardholder data.
  o Requirement 4: Encrypt transmission of cardholder data across open, public networks.
- **Maintain a vulnerability management programme.**
  o Requirement 5: Use and regularly update anti-virus software.
  o Requirement 6: Develop and maintain secure systems and applications.
- **Implement strong access control measures.**
  o Requirement 7: Restrict access to cardholder data by business need-to-know.
  o Requirement 8: Assign a unique ID to each person with computer access.

---

information or both. This also includes entities that provide services to merchants, services providers or members that control or could impact the security of cardholder data. Examples include managed service providers that provide managed firewalls, intrusion detection software and other services, as well as hosting providers and other entities. Entities that only provide communication links without access to the application layer of the communication link, such as telecommunications entities, are excluded.

    o Requirement 9: Restrict physical access to cardholder data.

- **Regularly monitor and test networks.**
  o Requirement 10: Track and monitor all access to network resources and cardholder data.
  o Requirement 11: Regularly test security systems and processes.

- **Maintain an information security policy.**

  o Requirement 12: Maintain a policy that addresses information security.

However, while the newly-established PCI Security Standards Council manages the underlying Data Security Standard, compliance requirements are set independently by individual payment card brands. While requirements vary between card networks, MasterCard's Site Data Protection Plan and Visa's Cardholder Information Security Programme are all representative. They stipulate separate compliance validation requirements for merchants and service providers, which vary depending on the size of the entity and its transaction/business throughput.

Summary of changes to latest version of PCI DSS

As you can imagine, the Standard is maturing and with that comes greater clarity and more specific direction on issues relating to 'how to comply' with the Standard.

Most of the changes pertain to clarification and in some cases 'more obvious' stipulations i.e. *'unprotected PANs should not be sent using end-user messaging technologies such as e-mail and instant messaging'*. Overall, more definition around 'testing procedures' and the use of other best practice sources, such as SANS CWE, CERT and, of course, OWASP, have been made.

The PCI Standards Council have also replaced 'employee' with 'onsite personnel' which is useful in our multi-regulatory environments. 'Company' has now been replaced with 'entity', thus I have changed all references to 'company and organisation' in the book to reflect this.

So, from these few examples you can see most of the changes were either clarification of words, technologies, phrases and examples, all of which have progressed since the Standard's last publication.

Note: The ranking of vulnerabilities, as defined in Requirement 6.2.a, is considered a best practice until 30 June 2012, after which it becomes a requirement.

Note: Updated note regarding use of WEP as of 30 June 2010.

Top Ten myths about PCI

It is worth remembering at this stage that PCI DSS specifies 12 requirements entailing many security technologies and robust business (operating) processes; most of these reflect common best practice for securing sensitive information, but some also specify very stringent requirements that need to be met and compliance demonstrated.

The potential scope of your compliant cardholder data environment may seem daunting – especially for smaller merchants who have little or immature, existing security processes, or entities that don't have endless amounts of IT professionals who can help guide them through what is required and what is not.

To complicate matters, some vendors, who sell security products or services, market their products in a broader context than just the PCI DSS requirements. This can make the process of becoming PCI compliant confusing; add this with the cost associated with compliance, and you end up believing many of the stories you hear about PCI. Thus, myths grow and can become mind-boggling if you don't seek some clarity around terminology and applicability. Once again, the PCI Security Standards Council has come to the rescue in order to dispel some of these myths by preparing the top ten common myths about PCI DSS.

Myth 1 – One vendor and product will make us compliant

Many vendors offer an array of software and services for PCI compliance. No single vendor or product, however, fully addresses all 12 requirements of PCI DSS. When marketing focuses on one product's capabilities and excludes positioning these with other requirements of PCI DSS, the resulting perception of a 'silver bullet' might lead some to believe that the point product provides 'compliance', when it's really implementing just one or a few pieces of the Standard. The PCI Security Standards Council urges merchants and processors to avoid focusing on point products for PCI security and compliance. Instead of relying on a single product or vendor, you should implement a holistic security strategy that focuses on the 'big picture' related to the intent of PCI DSS requirements.

Myth 2 – Outsourcing card processing makes us compliant

Outsourcing simplifies payment card processing but does not provide automatic compliance. Don't forget to address policies and procedures for cardholder transactions and data processing. Your business must protect cardholder data when you receive it, and process charge backs and refunds. You must also ensure that providers' applications and card payment terminals comply with respective PCI standards and do not store sensitive cardholder data. You should request a certificate of compliance annually from providers.

Myth 3 – PCI compliance is an IT project

The IT staff implements technical and operational aspects of PCI-related systems, but compliance to the payment brand's programs is much more than a 'project' with a beginning and end – it's an ongoing process of assessment, remediation and reporting. PCI compliance is a business issue that is best addressed by a multi-disciplinary team. The risks of compromise are financial and reputational, so they affect the whole entity. Be sure your business addresses policies and procedures as they apply to the entire card payment acceptance and processing workflow.

Myth 4 – PCI will make us secure

Successful completion of a system scan or assessment for PCI is but a snapshot in time. Security exploits are non-stop and get stronger every day, which is why PCI compliance efforts must be a continuous process of assessment and remediation to ensure safety of cardholder data.

Myth 5 – PCI is unreasonable; it requires too much

Most aspects of the PCI DSS are already a common best practice for security. The Standard also permits the option using compensating controls to meet some requirements. The Standard provides significant detail, which benefits merchants and processors by not leaving them to wonder, 'Where do I go from here?'. This scope and flexibility leads some to view PCI DSS as an effective standard for securing all sensitive information.

Myth 6 – PCI requires us to hire a Qualified Security Assessor

Because most large merchants have complex IT environments, many hire a QSA to glean their specialised value for on-site security assessments required by PCI DSS. The QSA also makes it easier to develop and get approval for a compensating control. However, PCI DSS provides the option of doing an internal assessment with an officer sign-off if your acquirer and/or merchant bank agrees. Mid-sized and smaller merchants may use the Self-Assessment Questionnaire found on the PCI SSC website to assess themselves.

Myth 7 – We don't take enough credit cards to be compliant

PCI compliance is required for any business that accepts payment cards – even if the quantity of transactions is just one.

Myth 8 – We completed a SAQ so we're compliant

Technically, this is true for merchants who are not required to do on-site assessments for PCI DSS compliance – for that particular moment in time when the Self-Assessment Questionnaire and associated vulnerability scan (if applicable) is completed. After that moment, only a postbreach forensic analysis can prove PCI compliance. But a bad system change can make you non-compliant in an instant. True security of cardholder data requires non-stop assessment and remediation to ensure that likelihood of a breach is kept as low as possible.

Myth 9 – PCI makes us store cardholder data

Both PCI DSS and the payment card brands strongly discourage storage of cardholder data by merchants and processors. There is no need, nor is it allowed, to store data from the magnetic stripe on the back of a payment card. If merchants or processors have a business reason to store front-card information, such as name and account number, PCI DSS requires this data to be encrypted or made otherwise unreadable.

Myth 10 – PCI is too hard

Understanding and implementing the 12 requirements of PCI DSS can seem daunting, especially for merchants without security or a large IT department. However, PCI DSS mostly calls for good, basic security. Even if there was no requirement for PCI compliance, the best practices for security contained in the Standard are steps that every business would want to take anyway to protect sensitive data and continuity of operations. There are many products and services available to help meet the requirements for security – and PCI compliance. When people say PCI is too hard, many really mean to say compliance is not cheap. The business risks and ultimate costs of non-compliance, however, can vastly exceed implementing PCI DSS, such as fines, legal fees, decreases in stock equity and, especially, lost business. Implementing PCI DSS should be part of a sound, basic enterprise security strategy, which requires making this activity part of your ongoing business plan and budget.

Why PCI?

Ensuring compliance with the PCI Standard is important for a number of reasons (listed below are just a few examples).

The first and perhaps the most significant reason to comply with PCI is because you have to. That is if your entity stores, processes, or transmits primary account numbers or data (PAN) i.e. credit card numbers, then your entity falls under PCI contractual requirements. So, despite PCI not being law (although a number of US states are making PCI legally binding), it is enforceable by the credit card brands through contractual penalties or sanctions; this could include revocation of the entity's right to accept or process credit card transactions.

These contracted and mandated security requirements apply to all system components, which are defined 'as any network component, server, or application that is included in or connected to the cardholder data environment' – this typically includes a large amount of IT equipment within a target environment (*see Chapter 2: Step 2 – Determine the Scope*).

To add clarity, according to PCI DSS, handling and protection requirements are specified and must be handled as shown in Figure 1:

Figure 1: PCI handling and protection requirements

		Data element	Storage permitted	Protection required	Render data unreadable
Cardholder data		Primary account number	Yes	Yes	Yes
		Cardholder name*	Yes	Yes*	No
		Service code*	Yes	Yes*	No
		Expiration date*	Yes	Yes*	No
	Sensitive authentication data**	Full magnetic stripe	No	n/a	n/a
		CVC2/CVV2/CID (3 digit code on reverse of card)	No	n/a	n/a
		PIN/PIN block	No	n/a	n/a

* These data elements must be protected if stored in conjunction with the PAN. This protection must be consistent with PCI DSS requirements for general protection of the cardholder environment. Additionally, other legislation (for example, related to consumer personal data protection, privacy, identity theft, or data security) may require specific protection of this data or proper disclosure of an entity's practices if consumer-related

personal data is being collected during the course of business. PCI DSS; however, does not apply if PANs are not stored, processed, or transmitted.

** Sensitive authentication data must not be stored subsequent to authorisation (even if encrypted).

Although Figure 1 stipulates which data entities can and cannot store, your entity should carefully consider whether or not it actually needs to store cardholder data in the first place i.e. a merchant may consider outsourcing the credit card payment process to a merchant hosting entity or payment provider (a service provider).

The second and perhaps the more fundamental reason as to why PCI was introduced in the first place was to protect 'us' (the 'consumer'), merchants and service providers from a variety of risks or 'threats'.

There are several types of threats that plague payment networks and according to the FBI, financial fraud is the second-largest category of hacking events on the Internet today. To support this, Gartner estimates that 20-30% of Global 1000 entities suffer exposure due to privacy mismanagement. The costs to recover from these mistakes could range from $5-20 million per entity.

What are the different types of threats (or vulnerabilities)?

The threat and vulnerability landscape* facing our entities is in a constant state of flux, with new threat types emerging and existing threats becoming ever more sophisticated. At first sight, it might be fair to say there is nothing ground breaking in this observation, as all security and IT professionals have lived with this situation for decades, but how vulnerable your environment is to those threats and what time difference between the threats becoming known (i.e. CERT) and the response (i.e. patch) required to fix them has become minimal. Such threats are known as 'Zero day attacks' and are now the threat of every entity connected using a computer.

** **Note:** The ranking of vulnerabilities (threats) as defined in Requirement 6.2.a is considered a best practice until June 30, 2012, after which it becomes a requirement.*

But we would not forget that many of the macro-environmental factors, such as political, legal, economic, socio-cultural and technical, that often go unnoticed, have greater significance for the types of threat that challenge information security and IT professionals daily.

These factors range from the well-publicised, such as the rise in incidents related to organised crime and increasing signs of internal misuse of information by employees concerned with job security, to the less obvious, such as entities outsourcing critical business services to entities that can help reduce costs, but which may not always be able to provide the level of protection expected.

The question of what actions entities should take, requires an approach that can flex with this dynamic threat landscape whilst maintaining value to the business. There is no silver bullet (and never will be) to selecting appropriate controls to mitigate all information security (and PCI) related threat types, but there are key areas of focus that entities need to consider – here are just a few examples:

Threat type 1: Information theft and leakage	The risk of cardholder data being stolen from unsecured databases by individuals or criminal entities is rampant. The US Federal Trade Commission estimates 27 million Americans had their identities compromised between 2000 and 2005.
Threat type 2: Brute force attack	This is the way hackers leverage computing power to breach security and in this case access cardholder data. Only real-time monitoring solutions can help quickly identify attacks and block them before any real damage occurs and another major credit card breach is announced.
Threat type 3: Insider breech	Recent statistical reports indicate that most security breaches are internal (as much as 70%), as staff on the inside are often privy to vast amounts of data, some of which could be cardholder data.
Threat type 4: Process and procedure control failures	Well-established policies and procedures are sometimes ignored in the normal course of business, such examples might include when sensitive data is taken home to be worked upon, or when data is not transferred following the correct procedures – a recent example being the UK HM Revenue and Customs transferring confidential data files from one site to another UK government department, sent on an unencrypted CD, and consequently lost in the post.
Threat type 5: Identity theft	Trying to protect against identity theft is one of the biggest challenges facing today's society, it is all too easy to obtain (fraudulently) someone else's information to be used against an unknowledgeable victim.

Threat type 6: Operating failures	The risk to some entities is often surrounding data leaving the site, such as back-up data, or this can simply be a lack of concentration that can quickly become the cause of catastrophic data loss e.g. back-up to wrong file server.

Unfortunately, should any of these threat types be exploited, not only do these security breaches put consumers at risk, they have serious consequences for the entities affected. According to Gartner, 42% of security related complaints involve credit card fraud. For each case of credit card fraud, the average cost to entities is £8,800 ($15,000), and IT departments spend an average of 175 hours on remediation after an incident. Additionally, reputational damage results in dwindling consumer trust and therefore can affect the bottom line.

To make matters worse, the negative publicity that accompanies any breach in security can be very damaging to an entity's image and share value. If you operate a business in California, you are required to disclose any security breach publicly under state regulation CA-1386, and as you can imagine, being forced to report publicly that credit card numbers have been stolen is one sure way to lose customers.

In fact, further studies from Forrester show that breaches in data security can result in the direct loss of up to 20 per cent of an existing customer base. This represents a significant figure to any size entity, and will end up hurting the bottom line and/or shareholder confidence.

The final reason for ensuring compliance with the PCI Standard is to avoid fines and additional regulatory scrutiny. Failure to comply with the PCI Data Security

Standard can result in fines that range from £100,000 to £300,000 ($500,000) per security breach, and in the States, the US Government can levy additional fines that can range from $5 million to $20 million.

To make matters worse, once an entity has failed a PCI audit, it is given an elevated risk status and becomes subject to more extensive PCI audits. The ultimate penalty can be a suspension of status and the loss of the ability to accept and process credit cards.

Just from these few examples, it is easier to understand and appreciate why the credit card brands got together to formulate the Payment Card Industry Data Security Standard. The appropriate treatment and use of confidential data has long been the plight of many security officers around the world, at last, the PCI has taken the first proactive (and bold) step to help regulate and constrain the loss of both consumer and business confidence and help reduce the level of losses being incurred by both business and the consumer.

How does PCI compliance work?

Unlike legal and regulatory compliance, such as the US Sarbanes-Oxley Act 2002 (monitored and enforced by the US Security and Exchange Commission – SEC), or the UK Data Protection Act 1998 (monitored and enforced by the UK Information Commissioner's Office) PCI is a 'contractual' requirement between the merchants and service providers, including hosting providers.[8]

At a fundamental level, any entity that comes into contact with credit card information must be in compliance with the PCI Data Security Standard. So there are no differing requirements for small, medium or large entities e.g. shops, clubs, online betting agencies, hotels, holiday entities, insurance entities, etc.

There are however, varying levels of compliance proof or validation required; each requiring different and very specific requirements for merchants and service providers, as well as various levels based on the number of transactions processed annually.

However, it is important to note that despite full compliance being mandatory, compliance requirements are set independently, by individual payment card brands i.e. Visa, MasterCard and Amex. Despite these potential differences, the merchant and service provider still have to demonstrate full compliance in order to process, store and undertake credit card transactions, so in the end it becomes a simple choice of if the merchant and service provider want to provide the facility of using a credit card, then they have to comply and demonstrate compliance with the PCI Standard at all times.

---

[8] **Hosting provider:** Offer various services to merchants and other service providers. Services range from simple to complex; from shared space on a server to a whole range of 'shopping cart' options; from payment applications to connections to payment gateways and processors; and for hosting dedicated to just one customer per server.

How is PCI compliance demonstrated?

In order to fully comply with the PCI Standard, every entity that the Standard applies to must implement all of the controls[9] (unless existing controls can be applied – also known as 'compensating controls') to the target environment and annually audit the effectiveness of the controls in place.

This requires the merchant and service provider to ensure that a formal validation and compliance (audit) structure is in place; and that validation requirements (including self-audits and vulnerability scans) are undertaken on a regular basis and results are fed into an information security management system[10] for ongoing review and improvement (e.g. PCI validation requirements are based on the number of transactions – the more transactions handled, the greater the quantity and detail of audits that are required).

Participating entities can be barred from processing credit card transactions, higher processing fees can be applied, and in the event of a serious security breach, fines of up to £300,000 ($500,000) can be levied for each instance of non-compliance. Since compliance validation requirements and enforcement measures are subject to change, merchants and service providers need to closely monitor the requirements of all card networks in which they participate.

---

[9] Compensating controls: Unless risk justified and compensating controls can be applied in full.
[10] Information security management system: For more information download ISO/IEC27001:2005 from *www.itgovernance.co.uk/products/139* or read the further information which is provided in this guide.

There are three types of validation requirements; these include:

1 **Annual on-site security audits** – MasterCard and Visa require the largest merchants (Level 1) and service providers (Levels 1 and 2) to have a yearly on-site compliance assessment performed by a certified third-party auditor, which is similar to an ISO27001 certification programme.

2 **Quarterly external network scans** – All merchants and service providers are required to have external network security scans performed quarterly by a certified third-party vendor. Scan requirements[11] are rigorous: all 65,535 ports must be scanned, all vulnerabilities detected of Level 3–5 severity must be remedied, and two reports must be issued – a technical report that details all vulnerabilities detected with solutions for remediation, and an executive summary report with a PCI approved compliance statement suitable for submission to acquiring banks for validation.

3 **Self-Assessment Questionnaires** – In lieu of an on-site audit, smaller merchants and service providers (Levels 2, 3 & 4) are required to complete a self-assessment questionnaire (SAQ) to document their security status. This is similar to ISO27001, as there should be a formal audit structure of scheduled audits that enables early

---

[11] PCI scans: PCI security scans are scans conducted over the Internet by an Approved Scanning Vendor (ASV). PCI security scans are an indispensable tool to be used in conjunction with a vulnerability management programme. Scans help identify vulnerabilities and misconfigurations of websites, applications, and information technology (IT) infrastructures with Internet-facing Internet protocol (IP) addresses.

identification of 'weak spots' and should feed into an existing 'enterprise risk structure' that enables the entity to fulfil other contractual, legal and regulatory requirements (regulatory requirements such as Basel II, SOX, Corporate Governance – Combined Code, US SEC, the UK FSA regulations and the EU Directive 95, Safe Habor, HIPPA and Data Protection Act 1998.

Under quarterly external network scans (heading 2) there are a number of additional requirements, that should be noted. In order to demonstrate compliance, the quarterly external scan must not contain high level vulnerabilities. The scan report must not contain any vulnerabilities that indicate features or configurations that are a PCI DSS violation. If these exist, the Approved Scanning Vendor (ASV) must consult with the entity to determine if these are, in fact, PCI DSS violations and therefore warrant a noncompliant scan report.

High-level vulnerabilities are designated as Level 3, 4, or 5 in Figure 2.

Figure 2 – Vulnerability severity levels

Level	Severity	Description
5	Urgent	Trojan Horses; file read and writes exploit; remote command execution.
4	Critical	Potential Trojan Horses; file read exploit.
3	High	Limited exploit of read; directory browsing; DoS.
2	Medium	Sensitive configuration information can be obtained by hackers.
1	Low	Information can be obtained by hackers on configuration.

- **Validation Enforcement** – While non-compliance penalties also vary among major credit card networks, they can be substantial. Participating entities can be barred from processing credit card transactions, higher processing fees can be applied and in the event of a serious security breach, fines of up to £300,000 or $500,000 can be levied for each instance of non-compliance.

Since compliance validation requirements and enforcement measures are subject to change, merchants and service providers should closely monitor the requirements of all card networks in which they participate.

Validation requirements

Implementing the compliance requirements is only the start of the process. PCI contains a set of validation requirements that are required to ensure that entities continue to meet the PCI Standard on an ongoing basis. The validation steps for the PCI DSS are described in Figure 3.

Figure 3 – Validation table

Level	Validation action	Validation by
1	Annual on-site PCI data security assessment and quarterly network scan	Qualified security assessor or internal auditor if signed by officer of the entity
2	Annual PCI self-assessment questionnaire and quarterly network scan	Approved scanning vendor Merchant
3	Annual PCI self-assessment questionnaire and quarterly network scan	Approved scanning vendor Merchant
4	Annual PCI self-assessment questionnaire and quarterly network scan	Approved scanning vendor Merchant

One important thing to note is that PCI have created security audit procedures (a tick box/checklist document) that provides information on the requirements for technical PCI compliance and also provides details on the expected content that should form part of the annual submission report – the 'Report on Compliance' (ROC) or 'Executive Summary Report'.

To assist the merchant or service provider in this compliance process an 'accreditation' scheme has been established. This has been designed to allow pre-approved PCI security and audit entities to offer 'Qualified Security Assessor' (i.e. auditor of system) services or Approved Security Vendors (i.e. penetration testers), or both. These services will appeal to the many merchants and service providers that need to comply on all levels with PCI DSS, but ultimately, every merchant or service provider will have the option of whom they choose to work with – in order to verify they meet all the technical requirements of PCI DSS.

Figure 4 – PCI DSS validation enforcement table

	Level	Criteria	On-site security audit	Self assessment question-naire	Network scan
SERVICE PROVIDER	1	All processors and all payment gateways	Required annually		Required quarterly
	2	Any service provider that is not in Level 1 and stores, processes or transmits more than 1 million accounts / transactions annually	Required annually		Required quarterly

	3	Any service provider that is not in Level 1 and stores, processes or transmits less than 1 million accounts / transactions annually		Required annually	Required quarterly
MERCHANT	1	Any merchant, regardless of acceptance channel, processing more than 6 million transactions per year – Any merchant that suffered a security breach, resulting in an account compromise	Required annually		Required quarterly
	2	Any merchant processing between 150,000 to 6 million transactions per year		Required annually	Required quarterly
	3	Any merchant processing between 20,000 to 150,000 transactions per year		Required annually	Required quarterly
	4	All other merchants not in Levels 1, 2, or 3, regardless of acceptance channel		Required annually	Required quarterly

For service providers, there are three levels of compliance. Level 1 encompasses members and non-members of all payment gateways. Level 2 is made up of service providers who process more than one million transactions annually, and Level 3 includes any service providers who are not in Level 1 and who do less than one million transactions in any given year. Therefore, audits for PCI compliance vary depending on a merchant's or service provider's level. A merchant that processes more than six million Visa transactions each year is assigned to 'Level 1', as is an entity that has experienced a security breach. Those at Level 1 are subject to significantly higher levels of scrutiny than merchants at Level 2, 3, or 4.

While PCI DSS non-compliance penalties also vary among major credit card brands (Amex, Visa, MasterCard), they can be substantial and, perhaps more worryingly, they can represent a major embarrassment and lead to reputation damage (which is difficult to quantify).

What is the role of the QSA?

Entities that validate an entity's adherence to PCI DSS requirements are known as Qualified Security Assessors (QSAs). Validation of these requirements by independent and qualified security entities is important to the effectiveness of PCI DSS. The quality, reliability, and consistency of a QSA's work provides confidence that cardholder data is adequately protected.

PCI DSS requirements, when implemented appropriately, provide a well-aimed defence against data exposure and compromise. As a result, on-site PCI DSS assessments performed by QSAs have become increasingly critical in today's complex online environment. The proficiency with which a QSA conducts an assessment can have a tremendous impact on the consistent and proper application of PCI measures and controls.

Each individual approved QSA will be trained by the PCI Security Standards Council regarding the underlying requirements of the PCI DSS and the evaluation of compensating controls for certain complex requirements and operating environments. QSAs will themselves determine whether a compensating control is sufficient, as they determine their recommendation of compliance to the various payment brands. Each individual payment brand will separately determine whether to accept the recommendation of compliance and whether a detailed review of the Report on Compliance (ROC) and compensating controls is warranted.

What is the role of the ASV?

Entities that validate adherence by performing vulnerability scans of Internet-facing environments of merchants and service providers are known as Approved Scanning Vendors (ASVs). The compliance tools applicable to Internet-facing systems include specific requirements for scans of merchants and service providers and periodic remote PCI scanning services of these entities by recognised scanning vendors. Validation of these requirements by independent and qualified security entities is important to ensure the effectiveness of PCI DSS. The quality, reliability, and consistency of an ASV's work is essential to ensure the protection of cardholder data.

Publicly available documents on PCI DSS for Approved Scanning Vendors v2[12] provides guidance and requirements applicable to ASVs in the framework of the PCI DSS and associated payment brand data protection programmes. Security scanning entities interested in providing scan services in conjunction with the PCI programme, must comply with the requirements set in this document and must successfully complete the PCI security scanning vendor testing and approval process.

Getting started with PCI

Nearly every aspect of PCI needs to start by establishing a baseline,[13] as each entity will need to understand where and if PCI is applicable; and what should be done to ensure compliance i.e. what the scope of the PCI target environment is.

As the security requirements of PCI extends to all system components that are connected to the cardholder data environment (scope), the scope of PCI compliance becomes extremely difficult to determine and therefore requires much effort and constant re-clarification.

---

[12] You can download this document from: *www.pcisecuritystandards.org/security_standards/supporting_documents_home.shtml*.

[13] **Baseline:** A baseline in most circumstances is used to measure the normal environment against a set of predetermined 'best practice' standards. Think of it as a minimum level of security required for operating an IT data centre – you'll need a building, electricity, water, floor capacity, environment controls, access controls, CCTV, etc. In PCI terms, this is what is required as a minimum level of security for handling, storing and transacting cardholder data.

Scoping the target environment is so critical that it should only be done by holding a series of scope workshops, in which senior management should be invited to contribute. The workshops also serve to better understand a holistic overview of the entire end-to-end business process, and thus, the scope is often not concluded, until completion of the gap analysis or risk analysis steps. Process mapping can also become a huge undertaking in itself, as understanding where the cardholder data traverses the network, infrastructure and file servers can easily become complex. Processes in themselves can also be complex, as often overlapping processes within a business are evident and yet all this needs to be understood up front to ensure adequate protection and eventual PCI compliance.

The gap analysis step can also be achieved by conducting a series of workshops or interviews. During which, the interviewer should seek to establish a thorough understanding of the level of compliance against existing policies, their supporting procedures and technical controls that have been employed (supporting evidence should be supplied). In addition, it is imperative that your entity can demonstrate it has identified all risks facing all its confidential data (and in this case – cardholder data) and how these risks have been analysed, addressed and/or mitigated i.e. accepted, transferred, avoided or treated – in line with PCI baseline (minimum recommend) controls.

The gap analysis can become very technical and detailed and therefore is recognised that sometimes, this level of analysis can be done more efficiently with the use of software automation tools.[14] That said, this only works if the entity has the ability to identify and report on the entire IT environment/estate – no easy feat in itself.

---

[14] **Software (data identification) automation tools (also known as Data Leak Prevention – DLP_:** Notwithstanding the need for conducting the policy, process and procedural gap analysis, it is worth considering an automated software solution as one of the ways to meet PCI compliance without a substantial investment of time and resources physically, as checking your IT estate can be achieved automatically (i.e. discovery tools) by using software automation and software compliance tools.

Figure 5 – Sample of components that need to be reviewed during PCI gap analysis

Policy:	Security	Access control	Logging & monitoring	Media handling	BCM & DR		HR vetting
Procedural:	Compliance	Logs	Review & reporting	Secure disposal	Back-up, recovery		New starter/leaver
Network components:	Firewalls	Switches	Routers	Wireless access points	Network appliances		Other security appliances, encryption devices
Servers:	Web	Authentication device	Database	Domain name service (DNS),	Proxy		Mail
Applications:	COTS	Custom apps	Internal web apps	External web apps / fulfilment	Finance (SAP)		Other apps (Snowdrop)

Certain vendor software solutions can also help cover critical infrastructure components, from operating systems, to network devices and firewalls, mail servers, application enablers and directory services by automatically collecting[15] hundreds of thousands of critical configuration settings needed to recover, secure, report on, and track infrastructure changes – all required under PCI.

Entities that can capture granular information about baseline variance and generate specific reports to demonstrate what is taking place in the environment have a distinct advantage over their peers. The consolidated change log report, for example, meets one of the key requirements of the PCI audit.

Much of this evidence provided by the interviewee, must then be further analysed, understood, reviewed and compared against PCI DSS (as the minimum baseline) culminating in the production of a PCI Gap Analysis Report. This report should detail where the scope of the PCI compliance requirement is (currently based on available information); and what can be done about any gaps found during the analysis (recommendations). This report should look to be an honest self-assessment of the entire (potential PCI) IT environment and include recommendations on how any policy, procedural and technical gaps can be filled by way of a roadmap and remediation plan (*see Chapter 8: Step 8 – Remediation Planning*).

---

[15] There are a large number of data automation collection tools, and some are extremely powerful, but can sometimes be difficult to configure.

Other related PCI Standards to take into consideration

Payment Application – Data Security Standard (PA-DSS)

One of the more demanding aspects of PCI is the requirement governing application security (Req.6.3), which mandates that you develop software applications based on industry best practice and incorporate information security throughout the software development lifecycle. Such techniques could include the possibility of using an ISO9001[16] based review process. Other alternatives include developing an approach to application development similar to those prescribed within TickIT,[17] and/or the governance process defined in COBIT.

PA-DSS v2 Section 5 – Develop secure payment applications requires all web applications to be developed based upon secure coding guidelines, and covered the prevention of common coding flaws such as the OWASP Top Ten, SANS CWE Top 25, CERT Secure Coding. However, PA-DSS v2 now requires all software applications to be developed based on industry best practices and a secure software development lifecycle (including load and performance testing) and ultimately – good configuration management. This therefore becomes the challenge (if it isn't already) of every IT operating environment. There simply is no easy way to avoid coding

---

[16] ISO9001 provides a number of requirements which an organisation needs to fulfil if it is to achieve customer satisfaction through consistent products and services which meet customer expectations.
[17] TickIT is about improving the quality of software and its application. COBIT For more information go to *www.tickit.org/*
www.isaca.org/Knowledge-Center/cobit/Pages/FAQ.aspx

issues, other than to address, specify and test (and test again) the inputs and outputs to ensure a clean code at the very beginning of the design stage – see also ISO27001:2005 – Appendix A10.9.2 On-line Transactions.

It is also worth pointing out that PCI v2, requires all web facing applications to have either a code review and/or a web application firewall, which will be costly especially if it is not budgeted or planned for. Other relevant standards that are applicable include:

• PIN Transaction Security (PTS) Point of Interaction (POI)
• Modular Security Requirements - v3.0
• Encrypting PIN Pad (EPP) Security Requirements - v2.1
• POS PIN Entry Device Security Requirements - v2.1
• Hardware Security Module (HSM) Security Requirements - v1.0
• Unattended Payment Terminal (UPT) Security Requirements - v1.0.

Despite there not being accepted industry best practice, below are some of references which may help your entity in its secure software development lifecycle:

• US Department of Homeland Security - Secure Software Development Life Cycle Processes[18]
• The Trustworthy Computing Security Development Lifecycle[19] (For Windows® applications – Microsoft have published The Security Development Lifecycle.)[20]

---

[18] *https://buildsecurityin.us-cert.gov/daisy/bsi/articles/knowledge/sdlc/326-BSI.html.*
[19] *http://msdn.microsoft.com/en-us/library/ms995349.aspx.*
[20] *http://msdn.microsoft.com/en-us/library/ms995349.aspx.*

- For Web applications – OWASP have published three 'How to Guides'.[21]
- For Java (and web) applications – Sun Microsystems provide training.[22]

PCI PTS

PIN Transaction Security refers to the framework within PCI standards and requirements that deals with the evaluation and approval of payment security devices.

Security is a never-ending race against potential attackers. As a result, it is necessary to regularly review, update, and improve the security development lifecycle and application requirements used to evaluate PIN entry devices and hardware security modules, collectively referred to as 'payment security devices'.

During 2009, the PCI Security Standards Council expanded its PIN Entry Device Security Requirements framework to cover two new types of devices: unattended payment terminals (UPTs) and hardware security modules (HSMs) under the PTS Standard.

Unattended payment terminals are an increasingly popular form of conducting payment transactions and are used in a variety of scenarios such as museum and concert ticketing, kiosks, automated fuel dispensers and car parking facilities. Hardware security modules are non-user facing devices

---

[21] *www.owasp.org/index.php/Web_Services*.
[22] *http://education.oracle.com/pls/web_prod-plq-dad/db_pages.getpage?page_id=315&p_org_id=1001&lang=US*.

used in PIN translation, payment card personalisation, data protection and e-commerce.

Both UPT and HSM hardware devices can now undergo a rigorous testing and approval process by Council labs to ensure they comply with the industry standards for securing sensitive cardholder account data at all points in the transaction process. The evaluation process includes the logical and physical security of each product. The Council will also provide a list of approved devices on its website, provide documentation and training for labs evaluating these devices and be the single source of information for device vendors and their customers

To gain approval by PCI Security Standards Council, PIN transaction security must now comply with the requirements and guidelines as specified and documented by the Council.

The PTS Security framework consists of the following manuals that contain the physical and logical security requirements for all payment security devices, as well as device management requirements for activity prior to initial key loading. The manuals listed below are specific to the particular payment security device approval class being evaluated, i.e. POS PED, HSM, UPT or EPP.

- Payment Card Industry (PCI) POS PIN Entry Device Security Requirements.
- Payment Card Industry (PCI) Encrypting PIN PAD (EPP) Security Requirements.
- Payment Card Industry (PCI) Unattended Payment Terminal (UPT) Security Requirements.
- Payment Card Industry (PCI) Hardware Security Module (HSM) Security Requirements.

For more information, or should you wish to understand this area of PCI compliance further, then please download the appropriate documents from the PCI Security Standards website: *www.pcisecuritystandards.org/security_standards/ped/inde x.shtml*.

Compensating controls – Using what you already have in place

This does not mean an entity can simply hide behind this get-out-of-jail 'clause' – it simply allows for any compensating controls i.e. controls that you already have in place on any of the 12 requirements, except for the storage of sensitive authentication data, BUT only if the control sufficiently mitigates the associated risk.[23]

Compensating controls may be considered for most PCI DSS requirements when an entity cannot meet a technical specification of a requirement, but has sufficiently mitigated the associated risk.

Therefore, you are required (on top of the risk analysis evidence) to provide and document the following: (see the publicly available documented example – PCI DSS Security Audit Procedures v2).[24]

---

[23] **Compensating controls:** Compensating controls may be considered for most PCI DSS requirements when an entity cannot meet a technical specification of a requirement, but has sufficiently mitigated the associated risk.
[24]*www.pcisecuritystandards.org/search/searchresults.html?s=audit+pr ocedures*.

1 Constraints precluding compliance with the original requirement.
2 Objective of requirement; objective met by control.
3 Risk – incurred by not using specified control.
4 Compensating control: how it meets objective; how it addresses any increased risk.

The effectiveness of a compensating control is dependent on the specifics of the environment in which the control is implemented, the surrounding security controls, and the configuration of the control. You should be aware that a particular compensating control will not be effective in all environments. Each compensating control must be thoroughly evaluated after implementation to ensure effectiveness.

An example of where a compensating control is often used can be found in Requirement 3.4 – Render Primary Account Number, at a minimum, unreadable anywhere it is stored.

For entities unable to render cardholder data unreadable (for example, by encryption) due to technical constraints or business limitations, compensating controls may be considered.

Entities that consider compensating controls for rendering cardholder data unreadable must understand the risk to the data posed by maintaining readable cardholder data. Generally, the controls must provide additional protection to mitigate any additional risk posed by maintaining readable cardholder data. The controls considered must be in addition to controls required in the PCI DSS, and must satisfy the 'compensating controls' definition in the PCI DSS Glossary.[25]

Compensating controls may consist of either a device or combination of devices, applications, and controls that meet all of the following conditions:

1 Provide additional segmentation/abstraction (for example, at the network-layer).
2 Provide ability to restrict access to cardholder data or databases based on the following criteria:

    a. IP address/Mac address.

    b. Application/service.

    c. User accounts/groups.

    d. Data type (packet filtering).

3 Restrict logical access to the database.

    a. Control logical access to the database independent of Active Directory or Lightweight Directory Access Protocol (LDAP).

4 Prevent/detect common application or database attacks (for example, SQL injection).

Therefore, only entities that have undertaken risk analysis and have legitimate technological or documented business constraints can consider the use of compensating controls to achieve compliance.

---

[25] *www.pcisecuritystandards.org/security_standards/glossary.shtml*.

A prioritised approach to compliance

The final consideration before getting started needs to be regarding a more prioritised approach to achieving PCI compliance.

The PCI Standards Council have come under pressure to help entities prioritise their approach to PCI, and as such, the table below provides six security milestones that will help merchants and other entities incrementally protect against the highest risk factors and escalating threats while on the road to PCI DSS compliance. The prioritised approach and its milestones are intended to provide an overview, which includes the following benefits:

- A roadmap that an entity can use to address its risks in priority order.
- A pragmatic approach that allows for 'quick wins'.
- Supports financial and operational planning.
- Promotes objective and measurable progress indicators.
- Helps promote consistency among Qualified Security Assessors.

The prioritised approach includes six milestones. The below summarises the high-level goals and intentions of each milestone:

Milestone 1

Remove sensitive authentication data and limit data retention. This milestone targets a key area of risk for entities that have been compromised. Remember – if sensitive authentication data and other cardholder data are not stored, the effects of a compromise will be greatly reduced. If you don't need it, don't store it.

Milestone 2

Protect the perimeter, internal, and wireless networks. This milestone targets controls for points of access to most compromises – the network or a wireless access point.

Milestone 3

Secure payment card applications. This milestone targets controls for applications, application processes, and application servers. Weaknesses in these areas offer easy prey for compromising systems and obtaining access to cardholder data.

Milestone 4

Monitor and control access to your systems. Controls for this milestone allow you to detect the who, what, when, and how concerning who is accessing your network and cardholder data environment.

Milestone 5

Protect stored cardholder data. For those entities that have analysed their business processes and determined that they must store Primary Account Numbers, Milestone Five targets key protections mechanisms for that stored data.

Milestone 6

Finalise remaining compliance efforts, and ensure all controls are in place. The intent of Milestone Six is to complete PCI DSS requirements and finalise all remaining related policies, procedures, and processes needed to protect the cardholder data environment.

Some strategic thoughts

It is well worth mentioning again that you'll need to ensure that senior management are fully committed and behind implementing the PCI DSS requirements. Failure here will lead to project delays and potential embarrassing non-compliance, notwithstanding the implications for your entity's reputation.

The same could be said for other legal and regulatory requirements – your entity will need to consider other compliance requirements that may affect you, such as: Sarbanes Oxley, Gramm-Leach-Bliley Act, Foreign Corrupt Practices Act of 1977, 1, Basel II, Health Insurance Portability and Accountability Act (HIPAA), Markets in Financial Instruments Directive (MiFID), Data Protection Act 1998, Combined Code, Computer Misuse Act, Regulation of Investigatory Powers Act 2000 (RIPA), etc – all require a level of evidence that security and a system of internal controls (usually achieved through combination of risk, financial and IT Control mechanisms) are being effectively managed and applied within your entity.

Furthermore, being PCI compliant may keep you out of jail – as some US states, such as Minnesota, are enacting laws that use PCI DSS requirements to define what information can and cannot be stored within a given environment. This effectively means that PCI can be used in those states, as either criminal defence or non-compliance may be used against your entity as evidence. As much of the US legislation and regulation ends up here, it is worth considering how our UK and/or European governments could potentially use this to become future legislation.

Conceptually, compliance with ISO27001 involves establishing an Information Security Management System (ISMS) to support the defined critical business processes, and then making any necessary security improvements within this scope to comply with the Standard. Within the context of the PCI project, the primary focus will be to establish an Information Security Management System that can manage ongoing risk, irrespective of source or motive and ensure appropriate controls are in place to provide consistent assurance to both the entity's entities and stakeholders.

It is also well worth considering that as PCI DSS applies to all system components that are in, or connected to, the cardholder data environment, reducing the size and complexity of that environment, may provide better security, achievable management, and limit the scope of your PCI compliance initiative. Whilst this may be non-trivial in some environments, it is usually well worth investigating (at the least) to see if your compliance requirements could be reduced to tolerable levels or, if outsourcing to a hosting provider should be seriously considered.

As previously mentioned, any legal, regulatory and/or contractual compliance requirements should be addressed not in isolation, but in unison with each other – ideally as part of an ongoing and operational ISMS. Each requirement may have its own objectives, but this usually boils down into the same few fundamentals – effective risk management, good logging and reporting, comprehensive monitoring and rigorous auditing.

Benefits of a combined approach to compliance

By combining the requirements of PCI DSS with the requirements of ISO27001 – Information Security Management Systems (ISMS) your overall defence mechanisms and internal control systems could provide significant business benefits and result in both PCI and ISO27001 compliance.

In addition, when combining PCI and ISO27001 audit steps, strategic business initiatives can achieve the information technology governance objectives as outlined in COSO,[26] COBIT[27] and ITIL.[28] So, in effect, your entity could have implemented the prescribed procedures as outlined in PCI, whilst simultaneously achieving compliance with other regulatory requirements such as Sarbanes-Oxley or the Combined Code.

The obvious benefit of this integrated and holistic approach is that entities and corporations will be able to demonstrate that they have good internal controls over financial processes (US SEC and UK FSA requirements), but even more importantly, that they can help mitigate for

---

[26] **COSO:** Internal control – integrated framework to assist companies in ensuring the effectiveness of their financial, operational, and compliance-related internal controls. *http://www.coso.org/resources.htm.*

[27] **COBIT**: COBIT is an IT governance framework and supporting toolset that allows managers to bridge the gap between control requirements, technical issues and business risks. *www.isaca.org/Template.cfm.*

[28] **ITIL**: IT Infrastructure Library –ITIL is the only consistent and comprehensive documentation of best practice for IT service management *www.itil-officialsite.com/AboutITIL/WhatisITIL.asp.*

information security threats before they become an incident.

Tip: In order to help your entity in this area of implementing a more holistic[29] approach to compliance, there is an international course that can provide help. The objective of this course is to provide you with the necessary skills to implement a corporate Information Security Management System (ISMS) framework that is compliant with the requirements of ISO27002, UK Data Protection Act, EU Directive on Privacy, HIPAA Security, , GLBA, Sarbanes-Oxley Act (Security), FACT Act, PCI Data Security, California SB-1386, OSFI, PIPEDA, PIPA, Canadian Bill C-198 and meets certification requirements of ISO27001.

This combined or integrated approach may also result in significant cost-savings – in some cases it has actually resulted in entities having a PCI (ROC) audit completed as well as obtaining ISO27001 certification; with little or minimal costs added during the same time period of your PCI compliance implementation programme!

This very cost-effective approach provides true value, because not only are such forward-thinking entities able to meet PCI driven requirements, but they will also be able to meet international best practice requirement for Information Security Management – and at the end of the day they will end up with a very strong, comprehensive and robust information security management system.

---

[29] **HISP**: Holistic Information Security Practitioner course: *www.hispcertification.org/*.

Background

As COBIT and COSO are internationally accepted IT governance frameworks, this combined approach could also save your entity time and money; and in the long-term, provide true value to your 'defence in depth' tactics by strengthening your overall security programme.

Other benefits include:

- A confirmed effective and risk justified PCI compliance programme.
- Effective COSO and corporate governance through a risk management framework that addresses information security, audit, legal and regulatory compliance.
- Justified security controls based on a formal risk assessment.
- Effective targeting of resources in the treatment of identified and related risks to PCI compliance.
- Reduction in the overall cost of information assurance delivered at a higher level of assurance in a higher level of collaboration – reduced cost of audits.
- Business focused and more appropriate policies and procedures.
- Good security awareness and a wider sense of ownership with clearer security responsibilities and accountability.
- Improved measurement of security control effectiveness through objective, independent assurance.
- Senior management assurance that information security controls are both auditable and being audited effectively.
- A single framework for many internal control initiatives.
- Reduced operational risk.
- Greater preparedness for emerging threats and vulnerabilities, whilst maximising the business opportunities from new technologies.
- Increased business efficiency.

- Closer integration of business continuity management, quality and information security initiatives to address business critical assets.
- Information security, quality and risk assurance to stakeholders.

The approach of this book

Below is the nine-step programme necessary to build a sustainable PCI compliance framework:

- Step 1 – Establishing the PCI project.
- Step 2 – Determine the scope.
- Step 3 – Review the information security policy.
- Step 4 – Conduct gap analysis.
- Step 5 – Conduct risk analysis.
- Step 6 – Establish the baseline.
- Step 7 – Auditing.
- Step 8 – Remediation planning.
- Step 9 – Maintaining and demonstrating compliance.

CHAPTER 1: STEP 1 – ESTABLISHING THE PCI PROJECT

One of the most important and often neglected tasks you should first consider is the project documentation. Any aspect of work that requires resource, time and effort, demands to be treated as a project in itself. Failure to follow this simple advice may lead to serious complications and worse – repercussions for your PCI compliance programme. PCI requires a serious amount of commitment and cannot be treated as business as usual.

To start, you should ensure an appropriately qualified project manager is assigned the task of overseeing the PCI programme. As any project manager will tell you, all the requirements of a project need to be assimilated and transposed in to a single document. This document is known as the Project Initiation Document (PID)[30] and can be used throughout the entire PCI compliance programme to ensure delivery of the original objective – PCI compliance. One of the most effective ways to ascertain all the pertinent information relating to the project is by hosting a project initiation workshop. This workshop will be essential in providing clear understanding for the basis of the project, and should provide a detailed breakdown of

---

[30] Project Initiation Document examples can be sought from many different sources:
www.ogc.gov.uk/documentation_and_templates_project_initiation_doc ument_pid.asp.
www.berr.gov.uk/aboutus/corporate/projectcentre/pm-templates/page12526.html.

the individual activities and resource requirements; including a definition of the deliverables and the success/quality criteria for a project to complete successfully.

What is the project initiation workshop objective?

The workshop should be attended by the PCI sponsor, the PCI team, the project manager, the security officer and other relevant IT staff who will be involved in confirming the scope of the PCI compliance (target environment) and the boundaries for the PCI compliance work.

The workshop objectives and therefore activities, should be discussed and agreed, some of these topics include (but are not limited to):

- The generic approach, as outlined in this guide.
- Confirm the objectives and terms of reference for the assignment.
- Confirm the boundary of the PCI compliance target environment and, where appropriate, the interface to third party service providers.
- Confirm the roles and responsibilities of people within the entity in relation to their responsibilities for security.
- Confirm the degree of management visibility of the work that the study will require including reporting requirements.
- Gain agreement on who should be interviewed and about what as part of the assignment, and whether or not workshops could be used to streamline the information gathering, stimulate discussion and raise awareness of the security improvement initiative.

- Confirm that a security improvement plan will be used throughout the lifecycle of the project to track, monitor and ensure the project is on target to achieve its objective – PCI compliance.

What are the workshop deliverables?

Following the workshop, the PID should be created:

1 A Project Initiation Document (PID), based on OGC, Department for Business Skills and Innovation[31], PRINCE 2 or APM[32] principles should form the basis of the control and execution of the project. The detail should be agreed between the PCI team and the project manager; and should contain:

    a. Define the objectives of the project work.

    b. Define the terms of reference and scope of the project work, in meeting the above objectives.

    c. Define the management structure, entity and associated responsibilities.

    d. Describe the proposed approach.

    e. Roles and responsibilities.

    f. Project plan, including key tasks and delivery dates.

    g. Interview list.

    h. Description of deliverables.

---

[31] *www.berr.gov.uk/aboutus/corporate/projectcentre/pm-templates/page12526.html.*
[32] *www.apm.org.uk/.*

    i.   Quality criteria by which each deliverable will be judged.

    j.   Any assumptions or dependencies.

    k.   Specify deliverables.

    l.   Identify assumptions and risks to the project.

    m. Identify constraints to the project.

    n.   Identify project and quality management mechanisms.

2 Also at the scoping stage, it is necessary to set out what the draft Security Improvement Plan (SIP) should look like and what it should contain. The SIP should be based on good examples (again freely available) and will be critical in contributing to the overall control and execution of the project (including during the project lifecycle and beyond). The SIP detail should also be agreed between the project sponsor, the project manager and the security officer and is the one document that will provide a continuous monitoring facility, during and after completion of the PCI implementation programme.

The SIP should look to contain at least the following components:

- 'No.' – Unique identification number.
- 'Relevant Section in PCI DSS' – the unique control reference within the Standard; this column may also contain the reference of the meeting where the action was raised (e.g. Project Update Meeting 1 – PUM #1).
- 'Description of Action' – description of work required.
- 'Owner' – the party responsible for initiating work communicating progress back to the ISF.

- 'Due date' – the target date for completion of the security improvement action; and
- 'Status' – the current status of the action; one of complete, in progress, pending, cancelled.

These aspects should be described to a level of detail that will enable your PCI team and participating staff involved in each activity, to effectively carry out their tasks, and should enable those who have responsibility for quality assurance to understand what is required of them and by when.

CHAPTER 2: STEP 2 – DETERMINE THE SCOPE

Once the initial project scoping workshop is complete, it is equally important to provide a clear understanding of the objectives and the scope for the PCI target environment.

Therefore, it is recommended that you hold another workshop. This workshop should be used to better understand the boundaries, exemptions, third parties relationships, and dependencies but it should be recognised that the scope will probably change from the start of the PCI project upon completion of the project.

It is important to note that an accurate scope is not only essential for your entity to gain maximum benefit from the PCI assessment but is imperative to ensure the project does not drag on for an indefinite amount of time causing it to stall or fail in its objectives.

Scoping the PCI target environment

Compliance with PCI DSS is concerned with securing any environment that comes into contact with cardholder data. This includes computer systems, business processes and networks that directly support or provide cardholder data processing, storage, or transmission. This includes protecting cardholder data during a particular business process or function of a third party where appropriate.

In order to be more manageable, the scope of the cardholder data environment would ideally be aligned with the entity's structure, and include only elements from a single legal entity. Other entities that are involved in the defined business process of managing cardholder data, e.g. outsourcing, hosting and service providers, cannot be considered as part of the PCI compliance scope, but need to be treated as key third parties and therefore managed through the risk analysis process with appropriate contracts (with adequate IT / Security Controls) in place. But first, let us clarify what PCI states:

The PCI DSS security requirements apply to all 'system components'. A system component is defined as any network component, server, or application that is included in or connected to the cardholder data environment. The cardholder data environment is that part of the network that possesses cardholder data or sensitive authentication data. Network components include but are not limited to firewalls, switches, routers, wireless access points, network appliances, and other security appliances. Server types include, but are not limited to the following: web, database, authentication, mail, proxy, network time protocol (NTP), and domain name server (DNS). Applications include all purchased and custom applications, including internal and external (Internet) applications.

Adequate network segmentation, which isolates systems that store, process, or transmit cardholder data from the rest of the network, may reduce the scope of the cardholder data environment. The assessor must verify that the segmentation is adequate to reduce the scope of the audit.

A service provider or merchant may use a third party provider to manage components such as routers, firewalls, databases, physical security, and/or servers. If so, there may be an impact on the security of the cardholder data environment.

The relevant services of the third party provider must be scrutinised either in:

1   Each of the third party provider's entities' PCI audits, or;
2   The third party provider's own PCI audit.

For service providers required to undergo an annual on-site review, compliance validation must be performed on all system components where cardholder data is stored, processed, or transmitted, unless otherwise specified.

For merchants required to undergo an annual on-site review, the scope of compliance validation is focused on any system(s) or system component(s) related to authorisation and settlement where cardholder data is stored, processed, or transmitted, including the following:

- All external connections into the merchant network (for example: employee remote access, payment card entity, third party access for processing, and maintenance).
- All connections to and from the authorisation and settlement environment (for example, connections for employee access or for devices such as firewalls and routers).
- Any data repositories outside of the authorisation and settlement environment where more than 500,000 account numbers are stored. Note: Even if some data repositories or systems are excluded from the audit, the merchant is still responsible for ensuring that all systems that store, process, or transmit cardholder data are compliant with the PCI DSS.
- An electronic point-of-sale (ePOS) environment – the place where a transaction is accepted at a merchant location (that is, retail store, restaurant, hotel property, petrol station, supermarket, or other ePOS location).

- If there is no external access to the merchant location (by Internet, wireless, virtual private network (VPN), dial-in, broadband, or publicly accessible machines such as kiosks), the ePOS environment may be excluded.

The approach used to determine the exact scope

Utilising the Project Initiation Document mentioned in Step 1, it is well worth holding a second workshop – the scoping workshop. The reason this should be held separately is twofold: 1) the attendees to this will probably be different to the sponsors and stakeholders involved in the project start-up workshop; 2) you want this workshop to be much more focused on technical procedures that support the business processes of cardholder data and therefore, the people involved with this workshop will help you understand the extent, nature and potential boundary of the PCI target environment:

- Describe best practice approach to all attendees and why they are invited.
- Understand the high-level objectives of the PCI requirements.
- Outline the work and resources involved.
- Identify key personnel and their availability for the initial assessment.
- Identify key risks and assumptions.
- Escalate reporting and communications channels (for issues to be resolved quickly).

Tip: During this workshop, it is well worth inviting the key decision makers/sponsors and stakeholders to the conclusion of your scope meeting. This will demonstrate you have a good understanding of their objectives and you should be able to communicate the PCI target environment (the scope), including locations and departments/divisions and people that need to be involved in the gap analysis.

Workshop objective:

The workshop should be attended by the PCI team, and all relevant staff who will be involved in confirming the scope of the PCI, in particular, you need to define and agree the exact boundaries of PCI (Note: this will probably change upon completion of the gap analysis and/or risk analysis work, so do not be too prescriptive with the definition of a boundary), before the gap analysis work can start.

The workshop objectives and therefore activities, should be discussed and agreed, some of these topics include (but are not limited to):

- Confirm the roles and responsibilities of people within the entity – in relation to their responsibilities for PCI compliance – including the project sponsor, stakeholders, security officers, risk owners, business process owners, HR, Legal, etc.
- Confirm who the project manager (programme lead) is and identify the team responsible for implementing any mitigating controls, policies and possibly – redefining or changing established business processes (as a result of the gap analysis).
- Agreeing on a defined approach for the gap analysis (akin to the scope).
- Confirm the objectives and terms of reference for the assignment.
- Confirm that for each phase, an outline of the work required should be defined, this should be agreed and

signed off by stakeholders or the project sponsor to ensure every deliverable for each phase is known and documented by all parties concerned to avoid confusion and project scope creep.

- Confirm the boundary of the PCI target environment (scope) and, where appropriate, the interfaces/dependencies with third parties e.g. service providers, hosting providers, any outsourced infrastructure, or for example if your entity uses a application service provider.
- Confirm the degree of management visibility of the work that the study will require, including escalation routes, reporting requirements – weekly, monthly.
- Confirm any commercials agreements, such as planned expenses, travel time and all relevant reward structures.
- Gain agreement on who should be interviewed and about what as part of the assignment, and whether or not workshops could be used to streamline the information gathering, stimulate discussion and raise awareness of the security improvement initiative.

Following the scoping workshop a scope document should be created:

1 A scope statement, detailing exactly what is in the scope on which formal PCI compliance will be applied for (ROC), and what is out. This is important because it sets the tone for the PID and should also include objectives of the PCI compliance. This document should also refer to the latest version of the Project Initiation Document (PID).

2 This document should also contain what is outside of PCI scope and why.

CHAPTER 3: STEP 3 – REVIEW THE INFORMATION SECURITY POLICY

As previous stated, there are six high-level and twelve sub-level objectives, and ironically, the final objective is the starting point of our compliance programme. Before engaging in the gap analysis and risk analysis process, it is important to understand what is contained and implied within the existing information security (IS) policy and what is required from the supporting policies and procedures i.e. anti-virus policy, user acceptance policy, HR vetting process and change management procedure.

This short but highly significant policy and its family set should be comprehensive and succinct as it will help you build the foundation for a comprehensive and effective information security management system (ISMS) and will ultimately help you achieve PCI compliance. Effective IS policies also help determine what assets and which critical business components support your PCI service and therefore which assets are considered business critical and within scope of the PCI programme.

You can tell a lot about an entity's attitude towards security by simply reading the IS policy. If there are gaps, then the process of reengineering an effective policy; including supporting policies, procedures and guidelines will benefit the entity hugely.

To start with, you need to compare the existing information security policy and ensure it:

- Identifies your entity's goals and objectives and ensures security is aligned to them.

- Protects the entity and employees from surprises and unwelcome audit findings.
- Provides the authority to endorse security activities, especially surrounding the activities of PCI compliance.
- Adds clarity for key roles and responsibilities; and therefore promote accountability.
- Is a basis for interpreting or resolving conflicts that might arise – if it is clearly laid down in a policy then it becomes difficult to dispute.
- Defines the elements, functions and scope of the security team and the responsibilities of every employee.
- Documents management's goals and objectives.
- Defines the response to US and EU laws, regulations (EU Privacy Directives) and standards of best practice i.e. ISO27001.
- Ensures that all employees and contractors are aware of the information security policy.
- Ensures that written documentation is in place for incident response and enforcement.
- Provides for exception handling, rewards and disciplinary procedures if and when needed.

If you do discover any gaps, or believe specific documents could do with updating, then, this is the time to capture these recommendations into the security improvement plan. This document will become key to the success of your PCI compliance programme, as it will soon be the place where you store and track gaps, risks and other recommendations that will come to light during the course of the programme.

CHAPTER 4: STEP 4 – CONDUCT GAP ANALYSIS

This activity is the information gathering and analysis part of the PCI project and relies on interviewing staff and assimilating information from existing policies, processes and supporting procedures and includes a technical review of systems, including:

- Network components, such as firewalls, switches, routers, wireless access points, network appliances and other security appliances.
- Servers, including: web, database, authentication, domain name service (DNS), mail, proxy, network time protocol (NTP).
- Applications such as all purchased and custom/bespoke applications, internal and external (Web) applications.

Business process analysis and reviews must be conducted with security management and support resources, business personnel, and other key stakeholders at appropriate levels to ensure minimum disruption to key staff. This will assist in identifying the core IT systems in scope and ensure that the fundamental business requirements for the infrastructure are captured and reviewed.

Gap analysis objectives

The objective of the gap analysis is to gain an understanding of the operation of the IT target environment from a business perspective and how any policies and supporting procedures, particularly in relation to access, installation and connectivity, could result in access to confidential cardholder data.

Therefore, the information gathered must be analysed to:

- Identify areas of compliance and non-compliance (based on PCI DSS and possibly ISO27001).
- Identify the key processes that have yet to be defined under PCI DSS.
- Identify the work that needs to be undertaken to achieve compliance with PCI DSS and prioritise accordingly.
- Develop a prioritised work programme for gaining PCI compliance by addressing the key processes and groups of controls required to implement and operate the PCI compliance programme (with realistic and cost-effective solutions).
- Highlight areas excluded from the review and why.
- Produce a brief description or high-level drawing of network topology and controls.
- Establish a list of individuals interviewed.
- Establish a list of documentation reviewed.

At the same time, information regarding the approach adopted for security management can be gathered. Additional interviews may be required to gauge the overall level of PCI compliance and how the different departments implement common security management and technical standards across the user base. Such analysis should look to include how information is reported to an information security working group/forum and whether there are office based nominees responsible (i.e. security officer) for security and risk within a geographically diverse entity e.g. France, UK, US.

Gap analysis approach

A simple approach that has been used in the industry for years can be employed to ensure that the key aspects of PCI compliance are considered against each relevant objective and are controlled within the Data Security Standard. This methodology is based on the assertion that true compliance requires the following aspects to be fully addressed for each of the 200 plus controls:

The following approach will help to ensure the information gathering is fully objective, repeatable and complete.

R – Is the person(s) who is *Responsible* for that aspect of delivery defined?

I – Are risked based controls or PCI based controls *Implemented* effectively?

D – Are the supporting procedures and policies *Documented* appropriately?

E – Can *Evidence* of effective implementation be made available?

The gap analysis will therefore examine the health of your entity's information security practices in all of the areas covered by PCI DSS, from the viewpoint of how they support the scope of the PCI and ultimately support the wider confidentially, integrity and availability requirements of your entity.

Some of the areas that need to be reviewed under the PCI gap analysis should include the following (not an exhaustive list) functions:

• Third parties (from a technical and physical access perspective).

- ISO9001 – to at least identify local functional gaps/requirements, establish and document necessary variants to high level horizontal business process.
- Information, configuration and asset management – including classification, handling and control (COBIT, ITIL and PCI DSS requirement).
- Communications and operations management.
- Localised and remote access control.
- Business continuity management and crisis management.
- Legal and regulatory compliance.
- Security incident management and reporting.
- Virus and mobile code management.
- Incident and problem management.
- Configuration management.
- Change control and change approval process.
- Security awareness, education and training.
- Personnel, HR and security vetting.
- Physical and environmental security.
- Systems development lifecycle and management.

Areas of compliance should be carefully documented such that the gap analysis report can be easily translated into a statement of applicability (SOA)[33]. This is particularly

---

[33] The statement of applicability (also known as an SOA) is a document which identifies the controls chosen for your environment, and explains how and why they are appropriate. The SOA is derived from the output of the risk assessment/ risk treatment plan and, if ISO27001 compliance is to be achieved, must directly relate the selected controls back to the original risks they are intended to mitigate. Normally the controls are selected from ISO17799, but it is possible to also include own controls. A number of sector specific schemes are being introduced which stipulate additional mandatory controls. The SOA should make reference to the policies, procedures or other documentation or systems

helpful, should your entity choose to demonstrate ISO27001 compliance at the same time.

PCI gap analysis reporting and security improvement plan

All gap analysis results and recommendations should be captured and presented in an information security improvement plan and should include the following:

- A security improvement plan (SIP) including detailed recommendations, time frames, resources required (this document will become your only way of tracking all the actions required throughout the PCI programme).
- A roadmap, indicating effort and time required to ensure all actions are resolved before PCI 'compliance' is achieved and by when (key milestones).
- Identification of areas of PCI non-compliance and clear guidance on what needs to be done to achieve compliance, highlighting appropriate recommendations with appropriate policy recommendations and cost-effective solutions (where appropriate).
- Any areas where compensating controls may be used – this will need to be validated during the next step – risk analysis.

---

through which the selected control will actually manifest. It is also good practice to document the justification of why those controls not selected were excluded.

CHAPTER 5: STEP 5 – CONDUCT RISK ANALYSIS

Before proceeding into the risk analysis step, it is worth clarifying what is meant by risk analysis and risk management. Risk management[34] is concerned with identifying, quantifying and managing the risks that can exist in any given environment. The risks related to key processes, people and key IT services should be identified and recorded in a risk register. These risks then need to be quantified and a decision made as to whether any actions need to be taken.

For this reason, the process of identifying, addressing and managing PCI related risks should be an integral part of every part of the PCI consideration and compliance programme.

Risk can be defined as:

'... the risk of direct or indirect loss resulting from inadequate or failed internal processes, people, and systems or from external events' Source: Basel II

Therefore, a concerted effort needs to be made to establish a risk-aware culture in which any PCI sponsor and/or implementation team will need to assess (and understand).

---

[34] **Risk management** is a systematic process of identifying, analysing and responding to project **risk** and risk analysis forms part of this process – it is often referred to under the more generic heading of risk 'management'. Risk management guidance can be downloaded from: www.theirm.org/.

Risk factors that should be taken into consideration include:

- What could go wrong?
- What is the probability of it happening?
- What would be the consequences?
- How can we reduce the probability of it happening?
- How can we reduce the impact if it did occur?
- How will we know that it is occurring or about to occur?
- What is our contingency plan if it does occur?

There are risks associated with all kinds of processes, functions, people – support teams and especially when deploying new technology. The PCI risk management process described in this guide provides a common methodology and focal point for identifying and managing these risks in a consistent and effective manner.

A number of other processes including IT service continuity management, availability management, configuration management, change management, problem and incident management and security management also perform risk analysis activities as part of their processes. Risk management provides a common structure for this analysis and allows the results to be combined and stored in a single repository i.e. a risk register.

The goal of the risk management process

The goal of good risk management is to ensure the continuity of processes and services by proactively identifying and managing the risks posed to them. This will include, for example, assessing the physical security of a building, the security (and safety) of staff, and not forgetting the confidentiality, integrity and availability of data stored within the building.

The benefits of risk management

The main benefits of performing risk management include:

- Risks are proactively identified instead of being ignored.
- Risks and their potential consequences are understood.
- Risks are prioritised so that the most effective use can be made of limited resources.
- Steps can be taken to reduce the likelihood of occurrence.
- Steps can be taken to reduce the potential consequences.
- Compensating controls can be risk justified.
- Measures can be put in place to allow early identification of occurrence, allowing contingency plans to be executed.
- Contingency plans can be developed in advance.
- A culture is developed where risks are openly identified and managed, rather than being 'hidden' from management.

The elements of the risk management process

The activities within risk management should typically include:

Step 1	Risk scoping meeting – identify and record high level risks.
Step 2	Desktop study – analyse and prioritise risks.
Step 3	Conduct interviews/workshops – conduct risk planning.
Step 4	Update risk register, monitor and track risks, react and control risks.
Step 5	Prepare risk management report.

Step 6   De-briefing meeting and presentation of the report.

The activities that will be undertaken for the assessment will follow the sequence described in Figure 6.

The success of the assessment will depend, to a large degree, on the briefing provided at the outset, the information available for the PCI project and the receptiveness of the project team members to the discipline of risk management.

5: Step 5 – Conduct Risk Analysis

**Figure 6 – PCI risk assessment methodology flowchart–
Original source: NIST[35]**

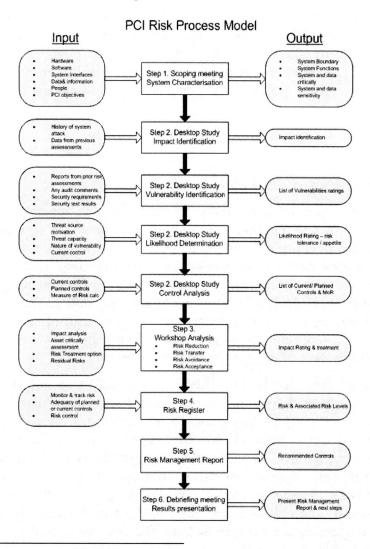

---

[35] *http://csrc.nist.gov/publications/nistpubs/800-30/sp800-30.pdf.*

Risk step 1 – Scoping meeting (identify and record high-level risks)

This step consists of scoping the boundaries of the risk analysis and identifying the current high level risks – especially those associated with PCI compliance. This includes describing risks accurately and recording them in a risk register (to be fully populated before external QSA visit).

There are two key tasks within this step, these are:

Task 1 – Risk (threat) identification

There are always risks present in the operational environment that threaten processes, functions, IT services and your entity's IT environment/estate. These risks need to be identified during workshops, brainstorming sessions, planning meetings, management meetings, team meetings, or by individuals in the course of their daily duties. The aim should be to identify, understand and above all promote a risk aware culture where risk identification is treated positively, and done as a matter of course.

Risks may also be identified as the result of specific risk analysis work within other processes such as availability and continuity management. To realise the full value of the process, risks should be identified at a specific level and not a generic level. For example, a generic risk might be 'hardware failure' which does not constitute the need to invoke disaster recovery, whereas a specific risk might identify the risk of a particular RAID (redundant array of independent disks) array and can therefore be treated as an isolated risk.

5: Step 5 – Conduct Risk Analysis

Task 2 – Risk (threat) description

Once a risk has been identified it must have a description recorded, so that it can be tracked. Risks must be recorded in the risk register.

For each risk in the risk register the following risk descriptions should be applied:

- Unique identifier for the risk.
- Risk description.
- Risk type.
- Risk owner.
- Details of who raised the risk and when.
- Analysis details including impact, likelihood and exposure.
- Any relevant timescales e.g. critical periods.
- Risk status.
- Mitigation plan status and owner.
- Triggers being monitored, including how and when this is occurring.
- Cross-references to any specific documents relevant to the risk e.g. the contingency plan for the risk, compensating controls, etc.

It is important that risks are properly described, so that everyone can understand the issue and the potential impacts. This is normally done by documenting the condition, the operational consequence and the business consequence. Specific risks should be categorised so that estimates of the various generic risks can be passed through the risk management process.

Risk step 2 – Desktop study – analyse and prioritise risks

In this step the risks are analysed to quantify them and to make sure that both the risk and its potential impact is truly understood.

Task 1 – Impact identification

Risks are normally determined by their nature – malicious, natural (Act of God), accidental, and their associated impacts. All these threat types should be identified in the very beginning of the risk assessment process and it is important to understand the potential impact on the entity (should they be realised).

An impact can be determined in terms of loss of customer, employee dissatisfaction, loss of shareholder or stakeholder confidence and the potential loss of business i.e. due to suspension of credit card facilities. These impacts should then be assigned a value on the scale of 1 (very low) to 5 (very high). To ensure consistency of approach across your entity, the impact scores should be in line with any existing business impact assessment that has been conducted in the past.

A chosen impact score should be multiplied by two to give an overall impact score; for example:

Figure 7 – Impact table

1	Very Low	Almost no impact in practice. If this has a financial impact then this impact will probably be well under £1M.
2	Low	Little impact in practice and the resulting issue will be dealt with and contained. If this has a financial impact then this impact will probably be between £1M and £2.5M.
3	Medium	This will cause some problems and could jeopardise delivery of the service/profile. The customer is likely to notice the impact of this. A financial impact would likely be in the range £2.5M to £10M.
4	High	Big trouble. Serious. The customer will definitely notice this and the resulting issue will almost certainly require and get director attention. If this has a financial impact then this impact will probably be between £10M and £20M.
5	Catastrophic	Threatens the viability of the service/project. Probably over £20M.

Task 2 – Vulnerability identification

How vulnerable an entity is to a risk (or threat) being realised much depends on its likelihood and potential vulnerability – for example; how vulnerable a server is to hard disk failure. These factors should be quantified using a pre-defined scale, and then used to calculate the risk exposure.

Vulnerability to individual risks on a scale of 1 (low) – 3 (high); for example:

Figure 8 – Vulnerability table

1	Low	If an identified risk was to occur, a low vulnerability level would mean that existing safeguards, such as controls, countermeasures or procedures would be sufficient to ward off the risk most of the time.
2	Medium	If an identified risk was to occur, a medium vulnerability level would mean that existing safeguards, such as controls, countermeasures or procedures would be sufficient to ward off the risk some of the time.
3	High	If an identified risk was to occur, a high vulnerability level would mean that existing safeguards, such as controls, countermeasures or procedures would be insufficient to ward off the risk.

5: Step 5 – Conduct Risk Analysis

Task 3 – Likelihood determination

This activity involves deciding whether the risk is significant enough to require action to be taken to mitigate it (i.e. how likely is server hard disk failure – dependent upon a number of factors and the number of times it has happened in the past). This should be done by taking into consideration the entity's risk exposure against a measure of risk appetite. The risk appetite[36] may vary between different entities, depending on the level of risk that is 'significant' to them. Where risks are felt to be significant, steps should be taken to mitigate them. Risks not felt to require any action at this time should be tracked to ensure that the exposure does not change.

Risks should be assessed for their probability, impact and vulnerability and scored according to Figure 9.

---

[36] Risk appetite: 'the amount of **risk** exposure, or potential adverse impact from an event, that the organisation is willing to accept/retain'. Look at: _www.coso.org/ERM-IntegratedFramework.htm_ and an excellent download is available from PWC: _www.pwc.co.uk/eng/publications/flash/journal-risk.html_.

Figure 9 – Likelihood table

Likelihood on a scale of 1 (low) – 5 (high); for example:

1	Very unlikely	Less than a 1 in 20 chance. Almost no chance of occurring.
2	Unlikely	Approx 5% to 20% likelihood. Approx 1 in 10 chance. Little chance.
3	Possible	Approx 20% to 70% chance. Approx 50/50 chance. Could occur.
4	Quite likely	70% to 90% certain that this will happen.
5	Very likely	Probably over 90% certain. Will almost certainly occur.

Task 4 – Control analysis

Risks are normally quantified by estimating the likelihood and potential impact of a vulnerability being exploited or occurring (i.e. server hard disk failure). Both of these factors should be quantified using a pre-defined scale, and then used to calculate the risk exposure. Other measures such as timescales are sometimes also factored in. This estimation may vary depending on the risk, but it is important to understand and document what existing or planned controls may be in place – as this will have a direct impact on the level of residual risk (and will influence which risks are to be treated).

Task 5 – Risk register

Once a risk has been estimated and evaluated in line with the above suggested tables, this information must be recorded in the risk register. Management information should be produced showing the significant risks. Individual teams or process owners should be aware of the significant risks affecting them and this will help facilitate the next stage – conduct risk planning – in a workshop setting.

A summary of the possible value ranges is provided below:

- Impact: 1 – 5   (Very Low to Very High)

- Likelihood: 1 – 5   (Very Low to Very High)

- Vulnerability: 1 – 3   (Low to High)

- Measure of Risk (MoR): 1 – 6   (Low to High)

The chosen scores should be then fed into the following risk calculation:

Measure of Risk (MoR) = (2*Impact + Likelihood + Vulnerability) / 3

As far as this is possible, the risk assessment should be carried out in alignment with existing entity risk assessment processes and scoring.

The aim is to ensure the risk registers (including treatment plans), which have been created as a risk management baseline, can be managed using a manual approach going forward.

Risk step 3 – Conduct risk planning

This step involves planning how to manage and mitigate the significant risks identified during steps 1 and 2; this should be done during a workshop (or an interview) environment to encourage greater user interaction and participation.

Decision

This activity involves deciding how each risk should be managed. This should involve formulating a mitigation plan, identifying whether a contingency plan is required, and identifying any triggers that can be monitored to provide early warning of the risk occurring. All mitigation actions must be cost justifiable (using quantitative analysis).

Mitigation actions may include the use of one or more of the following techniques:

- Risk reduction – taking steps to reduce either the likelihood of the risk occurring or the potential impact if it does occur.
- Risk transfer – transferring some or all of the risk to another party, possibly through the use of insurance or outsourcing.
- Risk avoidance – avoiding the risk altogether, often by stopping the planned action that the risk was associated with.
- Risk acceptance – taking a business decision to accept some or all of the risk. The decision must be taken at an appropriate level and documented.

Once actions have been agreed, resources should be allocated and timescales for mitigation/action agreed.

Risk treatment

This involves managing the implementation of the mitigation plan for a particular risk. If the risk cannot be removed in the short-term or there is to be a level of residual risk, then the mitigation actions will involve the production of a contingency plan for responding to the risk if it does occur. Risk treatment will also include setting up the monitoring of any triggers that have been identified.

Residual risk reporting

Once a risk has been treated, the residual risk needs to be reviewed and the risk register updated. The success of mitigation actions must be checked to confirm that they have achieved their intended objectives.

Risk step 4 – Update risk register, monitor and track risks

Monitor and tracking risks

The triggers that have been identified for each risk must be monitored so as to warn your entity when the risk is either occurring or just about to occur. Where possible the monitoring of triggers will be automated using software tools, but where this is not possible regular manual checks will need to be instigated. Risks and their exposures are likely to change over time, as other factors change both within your entity and externally. The risks need to be tracked so that these changes can be reflected in the risk register, and where necessary further analysis and mitigation planning carried out.

This is the ongoing activity of monitoring the risk conditions, consequences, exposure and triggers so that some controlling action can be taken if necessary; and is often neglected once the initial analysis has been undertaken. Where possible, the monitoring should be automated, but where this is not possible, manual checks will be required. The risks should be reviewed on a regular basis to ensure that they reflect the current situation/environment.

Risk control

This process involves taking controlling action as a result of a change detected during the monitoring and tracking of risks – as described in the previous steps.

Depending on the change detected, the following actions may be required:

- A trigger value has become true – raise incident record, invoke contingency plan, alert relevant staff.
- A risk has become irrelevant – retire the risk, but retain information.
- The condition or a consequence has changed – return to identifying and recording risks step.
- The probability or impact has changed – return to analyse and prioritise risks step.
- A mitigation plan is no longer on track – return to the conduct risk planning step.

In effect, this step involves further consultation with the entity to ensure the risks captured, identified and being treated are accurate, agreeable and appropriate to the entity's risk appetite and minimum PCI compliance requirements.

Risk step 5 – Prepare risk management report

This final step involves preparation of the risk management report which should be prepared in keeping with its intended audience (i.e. written using business terminology, not technical). This report is fundamental to the ongoing success of any PCI deployment and ongoing compliance programme and should be prepared in such a way that the recipient can continue to use it proactively.

In essence, the report should describe:

- The status of the project at the time of the assignment (including commentary on PCI scope definition, and any recommended scope amendment required).
- The findings of the interviews.
- The tools prepared for the workshop.
- The risks and opportunities captured during the workshop and their characteristics (in the form of a risk register).
- A description of the top ten risks.
- Identification of which mitigating factors can be used as compensating controls.
- The quantitative results (including source of statistics).
- The findings.
- The recommendations for further action.

Risk step 6 – Debriefing meeting and presentation of the risk report

The activities involved within the entire risk management process should include the key elements below. It is also important to reflect these during the final presentation back to the sponsor (presentation should be in PowerPoint and highlight key findings/recommendations derived from the report).

- How you identified and recorded the risks.
- How you analysed and prioritised the risks.
- What was proposed to plan and treat the risks identified.
- How you suggest risks are monitored and tracked going forward.
- How you can help towards controlling and managing risks in the future.
- What level of PCI compliance can be achieved if different risk mitigations are employed.
- How this might impact on the PCI compliance programme.

It is also at this point of the risk management process, that the benefits of using this approach to risk management should be re-emphasised. Finally, it is important to update the security improvement plan, as this document will become your only way of tracking all the gaps, recommendations and risks in one document (probably Excel).

Other benefits of conducting the risk management process include:

- Provides a more realistic outcome of the PCI project – risk justified.
- Increases a collective awareness of the risks, likely impact and the importance of taking proactive action.
- Establishes confidence levels in achieving the PCI project objectives.
- Provides an independent, impartial assessment of the current risk status.

- Enables realistic contingencies to be set – opportunity to enhance the utilisation of capital and time.
- Reduces volatility and provides greater predictability and enhanced profitability.
- Provides a roadmap of how things can move forward.
- Provides appropriate evidence for the Report on Compliance (ROC) to be submitted to the credit card brand provider i.e. Visa, MasterCard.

CHAPTER 6: STEP 6 – ESTABLISH THE BASELINE

The following chapter details what needs to be done in order to comply with the Standard as a minimum; it is not intended to be complete and should be used in the context of the previous steps – gap analysis and risk management. It is important to note that whilst this book provides some guidance on the interpretations of the PCI Data Security Standard, it should in no way be used in isolation. Therefore, it should be used in conjunction with the Standard and its supporting documentation.

Build and maintain a secure network

Task 1 (Requirement 1) – Install and maintain a firewall configuration to protect data

One of the most critical elements of the PCI Standard is the concept of separating the network and the systems that are involved with the processing and storage of cardholder data. Such devices include: firewalls, routers and switches, operating systems, database management systems and applications.

Under this requirement, it is essential that firewall configuration standards are set and that cardholder data is protected. One recommendation is to consider using VLANs[37] to physically isolate the traffic involved in credit

---

[37] A virtual LAN, commonly known as a VLAN, is a group of hosts with a common set of requirements that communicate as if they were attached to the same wire, regardless of their physical location. A

card processing, this would protect the cardholder data and ensure that only this part of the infrastructure is subject to PCI compliance scope i.e. target environment. You will also need to consider how you are going to demonstrate a solid change management process, so that any proposed changes to configurations, firewalls and routers are thoroughly reviewed and impact assessed, so that the impact of the changes is understood, documented and approved.

Tip: A good change management process will always include a back out plan (just in case things don't work out).

Tips for Requirement 1 – 'Install and maintain a firewall configuration to protect data':

1 Establish firewall configuration standards.
2 Deny all traffic from untrustworthy networks/hosts, except protocols necessary for cardholder data environment.
3 For any system component storing cardholder data:

    a. Restrict connections from publicly accessible servers.

    b. Prohibit direct public access from external networks.

4 Implement IP masquerading to prevent internal addresses being translated and revealed on Internet.

VLAN has the same attributes as a physical LAN, but it allows for end stations to be grouped together even if they are not located on the same LAN segment. Network reconfiguration can be done through software instead of physically relocating devices.

Task 2 (Requirement 2) – Do not use vendor-supplied defaults for system passwords and other security parameters

This second requirement may seem obvious, but it remains essential to evaluate all PCI-related IT components and generate lists of the default passwords, user IDs, and passwords. For example; in the Windows® environment, service accounts created under a system administrator's personal credentials are a good target for review.

You must take a holistic view of each layer and of every component that is involved in the PCI activity, and make sure that all the default system passwords have been disabled and the service accounts have either been disabled or that there is a legitimate reason for them to exist in the first place.

Tips for Requirement 2 – Do not use vendor-supplied defaults for system passwords and other security parameters:

1 Change vendor-supplied defaults before installation.
2 Develop configuration standards for all system components.
3 Encrypt all non-console administrative access.
4 Hosting providers must protect entity's hosted environment and data.

Protect cardholder data

Task 3 (Requirement 3) – Protect stored cardholder data

This requirement begins with the encryption of any information that concerns cardholder data. It is a very challenging requirement for many entities to meet, in part because of performance expectations and the complexities created by system integration. You will have to maintain a good track record of maintaining encryption mechanisms (cryptographic keys) and make sure there is a policy in place. Managing this requirement extends through the entire IT environment, from the point-of-sale or website to the data centre and thus can be very intensive.

Tips for Requirement 3 – Protect stored cardholder data:

1 Store as little cardholder data as possible.
2 Develop and test a data retention/disposal policy.
3 Do not store sensitive data (subsequent to authorisation) at all, even if encrypted.
4 Mask PAN when displayed.
5 Render PAN unreadable anywhere it is stored.
6 Protect encryption keys.
7 Document and implement all key management processes.

Task 4 (Requirement 4) – Encrypt transmission of cardholder data and sensitive information across public networks

This requirement ensures that any traffic going over the public Internet, whether inbound to or outbound from an entity's website, is encrypted. Entities may meet this requirement using a number of technologies, including Secure Socket Layer (SSL), IPSec, WPA and WPA2.

Tips for Requirement 4 – Encrypt transmission of cardholder data and sensitive information across public networks:

1 Use strong encryption and security protocols.
2 Never send unencrypted PANs by e-mail.

Maintain a vulnerability management programme

Task 5 (Requirement 5) – Use and regularly update anti-virus software

Anti-virus software provides the first line of defence; you need to ensure, and demonstrate, that the latest signature files are distributed regularly, to both entity-side and server-side systems.

Tips for Requirement 5 – Use and regularly update anti-virus software:

1   Deploy anti-virus malware software on all systems commonly affected.
2   Ensure current, active, and capable of logging.

Task 6 (Requirement 6) – Develop and maintain secure systems and applications

Under this requirement, your entity must ensure that the entire infrastructure involved in cardholder and credit card processing is updated as soon as security patches are provided. PCI auditors look for specific evidence that this practice is taking place in the target environment. Another part of this requirement mandates that adequate testing before a patch is applied to production systems takes place (think evidence) and that a solid change control process is in place for all systems and self-reconfigurations. PCI auditors are concerned with how frequently your entity upgrades applications, the quality processes involved, whether there is a traceability index, and whether they can pinpoint specifically what changes have been made to each application.

Tips for Requirement 6 – Develop and maintain secure systems and applications:

1 Install latest relevant vendor-supplied security patches within one month of notifications.
2 Have a process to identify new security vulnerabilities and update standards where relevant (this is also in line with Requirement 2).
3 Include information security best practices throughout the software development cycle.
4 Use stringent change control procedures and follow them.
5 Use secure coding guidelines for web application development (i.e. OWASP).
6 Protect all web-facing applications against known attacks.

Implement strong access control measures

Task 7 (Requirement 7) – Restrict access to cardholder data by business 'need-to know'

To meet this requirement, you must document each specific function in processing cardholder and credit card transactions and be able to demonstrate that each staff member performs the function allocated to that role only. You must also show who has access to which systems and data (i.e. role based access control). This separation of function helps to ensure that no one in your entity has access to the entire procedure for processing cardholder data.

Tips for Requirement 7 – Restrict access to cardholder data by business 'need-to-know':

1. Limit access to job role only.

2. Restrict user access by 'need-to-know' in multi-user systems.
3. Employ role based access control (RBAC) techniques.

Task 8 (Requirement 8) – Assign a unique ID to each person with computer access

Hopefully your entity already has a written information security policy in place, in some cases this is signed by each employee, but this is usually covered in employee contracts. Either way, it should state that all user IDs and credentials are to be used solely by the individual to whom they are assigned and for the task assigned to them (role). You should also ensure that they have a policy for password ageing and that password ageing can be verified and validated. For example, if your policy states that passwords should be changed every thirty days, they should be able to prove that passwords are actually changed within that timeframe.

In addition, you should be able to demonstrate that there is an automatic provisioning process in place for new recruits and for employees who transfer to other positions whilst still in your employment. In addition, the information security policy should state what the disciplinary procedures (or repercussions) are should a violation of policy occur.

Tips for Requirement 8 – Assign a unique ID to each person with computer access:

1 Assign unique user ID before granting system access.
2 Use authentication mechanisms to ensure correct person logging on.
3 Implement 2 factor authentication for remote users.

4 Encrypt all passwords during transmission and also whilst in storage.
5 Proper authentication and password management for non-consumer users and administrators.

Task 9 (Requirement 9) – Restrict physical access to cardholder data

To meet this requirement, you need to monitor access in sensitive areas, deploy procedures to track those who enter or leave the environment, and ensure that audit trails are stored in a safe location, in an encrypted format, and with good physical security.

Tips for Requirement 9 – Restrict physical access to cardholder data:

1 Employ stringent access entry controls to the facility.
2 Distinguish between visitors and employees (clear and coloured badges).
3 Ensure formal visitor handling, accompany all visitors.
4 Ensure visitor logs are retained and available following an incident.
5 Back-ups in a secure off-site location.
6 Physically secure all media with cardholder data.
7 Control media distribution.
8 Management approval of all media moved from secure areas.
9 Control storage and accessibility.
10 Destroy media with cardholder data when not needed.

Regularly monitor and test networks

Task 10 (Requirement 10) – Track and monitor all access to network resources and cardholder data

Under this requirement you must track and monitor all access to network resources and cardholder data – including during day-to-day, real-time, and dynamic events. To do so, you must have a clear policy about the kinds of data being logged and ensure the integrity of the data being logged. Importantly, and as per requirement 7, only those who 'need-to-know' should have access to cardholder data.

During a typical credit card transaction, log data is generated and flows through the network and is processed with business information, including payment authorisation, risk screening, fulfilment, and settlement. Hackers know that there are vulnerabilities in these processes that leave data unprotected. Internal threats such as insider misuse are also of great concern and therefore you should have an audit trail in place to be able to track and monitor unauthorised access.

Tips for Requirement 10 – Track and monitor all access to network resources and cardholder data:

1 Be able to identify who has access to what, especially with administration privileges.
2 Implement automated audit trails for all systems.
3 Ensure you have configured components to reconstruct specific events (for subsequent investigation).
4 Record audit trails for specific system events.
5 Ensure all servers and workstations are receiving regular time updates from a single synchronised clock server.
6 Secure audit trails to prevent alteration.

7 Review system logs daily and establish mechanism to escalate in an emergency.
8 Retain audit trails for one year minimum, with three months minimum available online.

Task 11 (Requirement 11) – Regularly test security systems and processes

To meet this requirement, you will need to demonstrate that your IT department regularly undertakes testing to ensure that all other requirements are met. The quarterly vulnerability scan, which focuses on penetration testing from the outside, comes into play here, as well as capabilities in place for integrity checking within your entity.

Tips for Requirement 11 – Regularly test security systems and processes:

1 Test networks annually, and test wireless at least quarterly.
2 Vulnerability scans at least quarterly and after significant network changes.
3 Penetration test at least annually and after major changes.
4 Use network and host-based IDS, and intrusion prevention software.
5 Deploy file integrity monitoring software.

Maintain an information security policy

Task 12 (Requirement 12) – Maintain a policy that addresses information security for employees and contractors

All the available Gartner and Forrester reports continually indicate that approximately only 30 per cent of entities have a written security policy in place. Yet as discussed in previous sections having a sound written information security policy (and its supporting policies) is the foundation for a solid information security management system. It is also essential to fulfilling the requirements of the PCI audit.

Tips for Requirement 12 – Maintain a policy that addresses information security for employees and contractors:

1 Establish, publish, maintain and disseminate a security policy that:

    a. Address all requirements in the PCI DSS.

    b. Includes annual processes identifying threats and vulnerabilities resulting in a formal risk assessment.

    c. Includes an annual review and updates when environment changes.

2 Develop daily operational security procedures.
3 Develop usage policies for critical employee-facing technologies.
4 Include clearly defined InfoSec responsibilities for all employees, contractors and third parties.
5 Assign responsibility for information security to one person or a team.
6 Implement a formal security awareness programme.

7 Screen potential employees and ensure references are validated.
8 Service providers must contractually adhere to the PCI DSS and accept responsibility for data held.
9 Implement an incident response plan.
10 Implement policies and procedures to manage all 'connected entities' and key third parties that provide outsourced arrangements.

Hopefully, this section has provided a flavour of the work required to ensure PCI compliance. There is still a lot to be done, but take heart that once the 'baseline' is achieved maintaining, monitoring and improving it should be straightforward, assuming you have followed the minimum guidance provided in this guide.

There is one last significant task that should be completed once the baseline has been achieved, and that is to update the security improvement plan. Don't forget that this document, having had significant input from the gap analysis and risk analysis, now needs to be updated to demonstrate progress and ongoing PCI improvement.

Tip: Don't forget to update the project plan and risk register as well.

CHAPTER 7: STEP 7 – AUDITING

The overall objective of auditing is to check over a specified regular audit period (which should last no more than one year) that all aspects of the PCI compliance programme are functioning as intended and that the minimum requirements, as specified in PCI DSS are being met.

Like many regulations, PCI can be intimidating because it is a broad-reaching set of requirements potentially including all of your information systems in scope. Unlike other regulations, PCI is highly prescriptive and there is a huge amount of supporting useful and free material available to help you determine if you need to comply; and therefore help your entity prepare for your external audit (QSA), external scan (ASV) or your self-assessment.

There are several activities that are essential to ensure that the PCI compliant environment continues to evolve and maintain its effectiveness in securing cardholder data.

These include:

1 Initiation of the audit (objectives and scope).
2 Auditor preparation.
3 Conduct the audit.
4 Report the findings.
5 Agree follow-up action and clearance of any findings.

Note: It is worth mentioning that whilst this section describes a generic approach to auditing, it is not intended to replace existing guidelines already provided. It is therefore recommended that you download, read and utilise the auditing guidelines freely available from the PCI DSS web site – PCI_audit_procedures_v2 and other good websites, such as ISACA.[38]

Initiation of the audit (objectives and scope)

What are the PCI auditing objectives?

Now that you have established your PCI compliance 'baseline', based on your SIP, policy update, gap analysis, and risk analysis a sufficient number of audits must be planned, so that the audit task is spread uniformly over the chosen period i.e. so that it doesn't come all at once.

As with any management system, auditing is paramount to ensuring its continued success, improvement and evolution. Audits play a major part in ensuring this validation and should provide sufficient evidence when inviting external auditors (QSA) for PCI compliance approval i.e. the ROC and the executive summary.

Note: The quantity of auditing is dependent upon the level of credit card transactions.

Therefore, the effective operation of the audit schedule should be in place to confirm:

- The information security policy is still an accurate reflection of the business requirements.
- An appropriate risk assessment methodology is being used.

---

[38] *www.isaca.org/Content/NavigationMenu/About_ISACA/Overview_an d_History/Overview_and_History.htm.*

- The documented procedures are being followed (i.e. within the scope of the PCI), and are meeting their desired objectives.
- Technical controls (e.g. firewalls, network access controls) are in place, are correctly configured and working as intended.
- The residual risks have been assessed correctly and are still acceptable to the management of the entity.
- The agreed actions from previous audits and reviews have been implemented.
- The PCI compliance programme is compliant with the PCI DSS Standard.
- That completion of the improvements/audit findings has been made.

Tip – The audits should involve reviewing samples of current documents and records; this should involve interviews with all staff, from senior management to shop floor employees.

Auditing objectives

The objective of auditing your own entity is to ensure initial and ongoing PCI compliance and to ensure a successful audit is conducted prior to any external auditors coming in (QSA).

Tip – It is better to find your own vulnerabilities/gaps then have someone else find them for you!

Therefore, your auditing objectives should look to include:

- An audit schedule – ideally as part of the original project initiation document (including scope of audit), but at least should include an annual breakdown of all audit dates and the areas to be reviewed.

- A set of prepared audit questions – prepare a set of audit questions in line with PCI and using ISO27001 or other good (and free) audit guidance documentation such as the ISACA guidelines for auditors[39].
- To be professional – ensure you conduct the audits (business processes and technical) within all appropriate business and IT areas and be polite.
- Audit deliverables – produce an audit report and conduct feedback meetings (to discuss findings, recommendations and improvements) and make sure you retain the evidence to back up your findings (including compliant and non-compliant).
- Preparation – help your entity prepare for external PCI compliance and any simultaneous certification audits i.e. ISO27001, by holding a series of seminars and communication notices (including dos and don'ts).

Tip: Make sure you notify the relevant areas when they will be audited, this will ensure cooperation and adequate preparation (nobody likes surprises).

Technical audit objectives

The objective is to provide a fully auditable and traceable exploration and test programme as required under PCI DSS. This allows any issues identified to be validated and rated before being rectified. It also allows for any penetration test

---

[39] *www.isaca.org/Knowledge-Center/Standards/Pages/default.aspx* for IS auditing.

to be repeated, ensuring that the corrective action taken has had the required results.

Therefore, the objective of the technical audit is to gather background information, and specify technical solutions that will help rectify or mitigate any potential technical failures (risks/vulnerabilities) from a PCI DSS compatibility perspective.

Scope

Each audit should be used to determine both the adequacy of its part in contributing towards PCI compliance and how it helps to achieve the PCI objectives effectively (i.e. secure cardholder configuration database, secure user working practices). Ultimately, PCI audit and compliance should be built into the existing audit processes and procedures, using auditing as a way to measure your level of PCI compliance (possibly using a dashboard effect).

Tip: Don't forget the continuing accuracy of the PCI compliance must be included with the report on compliance submission.

Auditor preparation

When assessing compliance against the PCI Standard, it is essential to examine whether the items that should have been produced in accordance with the PCI DSS, were available (e.g. evidence of logs and records). If there are deviations from the requirements laid down in the PCI Standard, the audit team should attempt to determine the causes and help suggest ways to avoid these potential issues.

It is conceivable that some parts of the Standard are never used. In these cases the audit team should consider whether the unused part of the PCI is still relevant, and if not, make a recommendation on whether it should be removed from the ROC.

The auditor may select a representative sample of system components to test. The sample must be a representative selection of all of the types of system components, and include a variety of operating systems, functions, and applications that are applicable to the area being reviewed. For example, the reviewer could choose Sun servers running Apache WWW, NT servers running Oracle, mainframe systems running legacy card processing applications, data transfer servers running HP-UX, and Linux Servers running MYSQL. If all applications run from a single operating system (for example, NT, Sun), then the sample should still include a variety of applications (for example, database servers, web servers, data transfer servers).

In addition to the PCI auditing requirements set out in the PCI_Audit_Procedures v2, the following information can be used to help when auditing against the Standard.

Technical audit preparation

Technical audits can be achieved by:

1 Conducting interviews with appropriate personnel as nominated by IT management. These interviews should be used to gather information on technical background, threats and vulnerabilities, business impacts, and general security management.

2 Where available, review existing documentation to determine network or application architecture.
3 Review other pertinent information relevant to those services being supported by external third parties.
4 Automated IP discovery tools. These IP discovery scans should be able to provide a further vulnerability assessment of devices against known operating system and applications security vulnerabilities.
5 Manual inspection of specific device configuration. This should provide the technical auditor with assurance that information supplied during the interview, coupled with the details provided in the documentation, was current and can be verified.

As it is recognised that whilst the use of testing tools provides assurance against basic attempts to circumvent the security mechanisms designed to protect the system, more in-depth analysis by skilled, trained practitioners should augment this process, as many of the attacks that are known, would not be detected by simply using a vulnerability scanning tool.

A number of non-intrusive vulnerability scans of the network and network elements using industry recognised tools must also be performed. This work should involve technical network mapping, system interrogation and some aspects of security assessment.

Where firewall systems and intrusion detection and prevention tools are deployed, it may be necessary to have connections on each separate leg, to enable scanning traffic to reach all connected systems.

Conduct the audit

There are many areas to be reviewed during the auditing process and the PCI provided guides should not be used exclusively when conducting audits. The following sections provide some sample areas that will help determine the maturity of the security management practices within your entity (ideally – this list should be refined and agreed during the scoping workshop) and help you manage PCI compliance going forward:

There are seven components and their supporting functions that need to be reviewed during the auditing process. These include:

Task 1) Review the information security management system components

- Visible management commitment to information security.
- Identification of business and security objectives as well as legal, regulatory and contractual requirements for compliance.
- Risk management and assessment.
- Control selection process.
- Internal auditing (including technical penetration assessments).
- Performance and effectiveness measurement.
- Management review processes (continuous improvement).
- Security improvement programme.
- Communication and enforcement of minimum standards across the estate.

Task 2) Review policy components

For all policies listed below, associated processes, procedures and standards may also need to be reviewed and therefore audited against, including:

- Information security policy.
- Acceptable use policies (including use of e-mail for sensitive information).
- Data retention and disposal policies.
- Data classification and labelling policies (specifically classification of UK Visa application data).
- Password policies.
- Access control policies (logical access).
- Third party access policies.
- Physical access control policies (physical access).
- Physical storage and media handling policies (including evidence of inventory).
- Anti-virus and malicious code policies.
- Patching and vulnerability management policies.
- System testing policies.
- Any code of connection (required for UK government departments).

Task 3) Review the process functions

- HR process.
- Business justified Role Based Access Control (RBAC).
- Documented information security roles and responsibilities.
- Entity of information security (e.g. management responsibilities and entity charts).
- Security awareness programmes and training.

- Screening of staff (employees and contractors).
- Contract clauses with service providers.
- Change management.
- Incident response provisions, including:
  o Incident management.
  o Disaster recovery.
  o Business continuity and crisis management.
  o Fraud detection and subsequent investigations.
- Log analysis and retention.
- Application testing and acceptance process.
- Security testing procedures.

Task 4) Review the procedure components

- Operational security procedures.
- Back-up and retrieval procedure.
- Procedures for all of the above policies and processes.

Task 5) Review the standards

- Secure build standards.
- Hardening standards.
- System development lifecycle management.
- Website design standards.
- Security architecture standard.
- Secure coding standards.
- Application development standards, including:
  o Web application standards.
  o Portable device standards.
  o Database standards.
  o Independent verification standards.

Task 6) Review the user management

During the audit review, the application and implementation of user and account management policies needs to be examined and reviewed for accuracy. This is usually carried out by interviewing staff responsible for the technical environment.

It is also imperative that you review the access controls around third party access to your infrastructure and systems i.e. for remote support, maintenance and upgrades. This should include reviewing and auditing:

- Provisioning of new user accounts.
- Deletion of old and unused accounts.
- Password management.
- Appropriate use of strong authentication / 2 factor authentication.
- Use of RADIUS/TACACS where necessary.
- Use of administrator accounts (specifically access to system components).
- Audit and accountability, including audit policies and synchronisation of system clocks and audit logs
- Storage of audit logs.

Task 7) Review the technical components

A detailed technical audit of specific critical network systems (such as core switches and routers) and representative devices (where many are configured similarly) through manual inspection of configuration files and access policies must be conducted. This task should focus on understanding the operation of the network elements that provide core switching functions, external access points and security devices including firewalls and how this all hangs together within the target (cardholder data) environment.

This review should not be limited to the target environment (cardholder data), as vulnerabilities found in other adjacent networks (for example: within the VLAN), may be used to exploit or launch an attack on the target. Technical analysis should, as a minimum, include each of the following areas of review:

- Network configuration including servers, routers, switches, firewalls, and remote access facilities.
- Virus protection.
- Internal network security.
- Network management, maintenance and operational support.
- Content management (SMTP/HTTP/FTP).
- Laptop and desktop security.
- Security of existing handheld devices e.g. PDA/Blackberry.
- Review current plans for securing USB connectivity.
- Mobile e-mail services including personal accounts.
- Emerging technologies such as wireless.
- Any arrangements in support of the PCI compliance programme.
- Technical regulatory requirements such as SOX or the DPA.

Validating that your systems meet the technical criteria of the PCI requirements is no easy task, therefore if you don't already have technical vulnerability expertise within your entity, or you wish to be totally impartial, then the role (and relationship) with your chosen approved scanning vendor or qualified security assessor, becomes crucial.

Report the findings

Audit reporting

During the reporting phase, management and the PCI sponsors need to receive formal feedback from the audit team. This knowledge transfer should be an open and transparent process. Almost every audit identifies opportunities for improvement.

Audit deliverables

The audit results and recommendations must be captured and presented in the following format:

- Audit improvement plan that feeds into the security improvement plan.
- Technical updates to the report on compliance.
- This audit should not only identify areas of non-compliance, but also provide clear guidance as to what needs to be done to achieve compliance, in a given timeframe and by highlighting appropriate recommendations, with appropriate technical solutions.
- Inputs into the risk register.

The above approach should ensure a skills transfer to enable key personnel to carry on, for instance, with the audits in the future. This element of the PCI project also requires multiple templates for all auditing checklists to be completed in advance; this will enable your entity to continue auditing well into the future.

Agree follow-up action and clearance of any findings

The primary goal of management and auditors should be to address critical issues first, followed by important issues. Both management and auditors should work to ensure that, whatever action plans they set, the goals are achievable and beneficial to the entity.

During the reporting phase, management must determine which corrective actions it will implement and when, based on audit findings. Managers must provide oversight and support to ensure the timely resolution of found issues. Although the audit team may make recommendations based on its assessments of risks and their consequences facing the entity, it should not make or dictate managerial decisions. The objective of the audit is to identify, inform and provide recommended ways to resolve and close any gaps found.

CHAPTER 8: STEP 8 – REMEDIATION PLANNING

The remediation plan will integrate all findings from each of the assessments (gap, risk, establishing the baseline and audits) to build a combined remediation plan (also known as SIP). Once again, it is well worth assigning experienced and qualified project managers to build a remediation plan; ensuring key stakeholders and sponsors form part of a project review board.

The project manager should develop and deliver the project documentation that will demonstrate the rigour of all the processes described in the previous sections and should outline a clear roadmap on how to deliver the PCI compliance plan within the agreed scope and timeframes.

As a minimum, the remediation plan should include the following:

- Project start-up and mobilisation of key business stakeholders/sponsors.
- Production of a project plan i.e. Gantt chart.
- A detailed remediation plan incorporating all of the findings and what is proposed to be done about them.
- Allocation of follow-on actions to named individuals.
- Time frames for fixing/resolving the findings.
- The remediation plan should also be presented to key stakeholders, the sponsor and senior management.
- How once implemented, your entity will continue to demonstrate PCI compliance.
- Comparison to the security improvement plan and how each will run concurrently.

Once developed, the project should be handed over to a business/department manager, who would be responsible to implement the recommendations and provide business-as-usual compliance functions required e.g. audit, improvement, pen testing.

Tip: Whilst the remediation plan will specifically address the issues of PCI compliance, providing, in effect, a project plan of improvements, the SIP should continue to be used as the master document that tracks all improvements, including lessons learned from incidents, audit results (both internal and external) and, therefore, should be used as the basis for continuous improvement of your information security management system.

Figure 10 – An example of a PCI compliance programme time line (6-9 months)

CHAPTER 9: STEP 9 – MAINTAINING AND DEMONSTRATING COMPLIANCE

Maintaining regulatory compliance requires your entity to be able to demonstrate that the systems are secure, and that adequate processes and procedures are in place to quickly address any gaps in your security posture. For publicly traded entities, this can include detailed reports for financial systems as required by Sarbanes-Oxley (SOX) and corporate governance requirements detailed in the Combined Code 2006.

All entities need to contend with the growing in number and complexity of legal and regulatory compliance – irrespective of size. FISMA (US), SoX, the Data Protection Act[40], the European Directive, California SB 1386 (US); and of course the Payment Card Data Security Standard (PCI DSS). All require significant commitment that controls are being employed and that these controls are adequate and appropriate to the risks identified and managed.

This, effectively, means that almost every entity – irrespective of the complexity, size, or contractual/regulatory requirements – has to ensure that a set of rigorous security requirements are addressed, maintained, monitored and improved.

In essence, you will need to seriously consider what mechanisms you plan to use to manage all of this information. It is therefore recommended that you consider

---

[40] Data Protection Act: *www.ico.gov.uk/what_we_cover.aspx*.

using best practice guidance in the form of ISO27002 (ISO17799) Code of Practice to formulate the basis of this management system.

Before you consider some of the solutions that will help deliver compliance, it is worth reminding ourselves of the validation requirements as ultimately this drives all the PCI requirements in the first place.

Items such as log storage size and what reporting is required deserve careful consideration and may need a project set up specifically for this requirement.

Validation requirements

Implementing the compliance requirements is only the start of the process. PCI contains a set of validation requirements that are required to ensure that entities continue to meet the PCI Standard on an ongoing basis. The validation required for PCI DSS is described in Figures 11 and 12.

Figure 11 – Validation action table (levels are based on volume and/or risk)

Level	Validation action	Validation by
1	Annual on-site PCI data security assessment and quarterly network scan	Qualified security assessor or internal auditor if signed by officer of the entity
2	Annual PCI self-assessment questionnaire and quarterly network scan	Approved scanning vendor Merchant
3	Annual PCI self-assessment questionnaire and quarterly network scan	Approved scanning vendor Merchant
4	Annual PCI self-assessment questionnaire and quarterly network scan	Approved scanning vendor Merchant

Figure 12 – Merchant/service provider category table

Level	Description
Merchant Level 1	Any merchant – regardless of acceptance channel – processing over 6,000,000 Visa transactions per year. Any merchant that has suffered a hack or an attack that resulted in an account data compromise. Any merchant that Visa, at its sole discretion, determines should meet the Level 1 merchant requirements to minimise risk to the Visa system. Any merchant identified by any other payment card brand as Level 1.
Merchant Level 2	Any merchant – regardless of acceptance channel – processing 1,000,000 to 6,000,000 Visa transactions per year.
Merchant Level 3	Any merchant processing 20,000 to 1,000,000 Visa e-commerce transactions per year.
Merchant Level 4	Any merchant processing fewer than 20,000 Visa e-commerce transactions per year, and all other merchants – regardless of acceptance channel – processing up to 1,000,000 Visa transactions per year.

Service provider Level 1	All Visa Net processors (member and non-member) and all payment gateways.
Service provider Level 2	Any service provider that is not in Level 1 and stores, processes, or transmits more than 1,000,000 Visa accounts/transactions annually.
Service provider Level 3	Any service provider that is not in Level 1 and stores, processes, or transmits fewer than 1,000,000 Visa accounts/transactions annually.

How to meet these requirements

This is possibly one of the more difficult (and sometimes neglected) requirements of PCI compliance. Vast swathes of information are required to remain compliant and an entire log management and SAN solution may be required just to ensure the appropriate log information is readily available at the time of audit. That is to say, that despite having all the basic elements of an operational ISMS in place, such as:

- IS policy set.
- Scope.
- Gap analysis mechanism.
- Risk management documentation (risk register).
- Security improvement plan.
- Problem and incident management.
- Change management.
- Documented operational procedures.
- Audit schedules.
- Business continuity plans.

You still need to consider the use of log management and automation tools in order to help generate compliance and log reports. This is basically because managing PCI compliance and capturing appropriate log information across your IT estate can be extremely difficult. In fact it can make or break your compliance!

Using log management information for PCI compliance

A comprehensive log management information[41] (often referred to as LMI) solution that can collect, aggregate and centrally store all data from network devices and server entities could be extremely beneficial to meet the goals of the PCI Standard.

LMI should help provide security, identity access and change management, and monitoring capabilities necessary to comply with PCI and other similar standards ISO27001, ITIL, COBIT.

To implement a log management solution capable of satisfying PCI requirements, it is worth considering the following:

- Does the log management strategy align with corporate business objectives and IT goals?

---

[41] There are various LMI products available: LogLogic and Guidance Software have similar tools to help analyse data, either of which can help simplify your PCI compliance requirements. *www.loglogic.com* or Guidance Software EnCase eDiscovery tool – *www.guidancesoftware.com/ediscovery-software-frcp-inside-counsel.htm?*.

- Will establishing IT controls and processes that enforce these goals help or hinder the PCI compliance programme?
- How will your entity securely transmit all data collected from these logs to a central repository?
- Is there a solution that offers the ability to easily search through, report on and set alerts on the data?
- Will automating the log management processes and reporting requirement actually benefit your entity?
- Store data in its original, unaltered format, so that it is more credible in legal and compliance investigations.
- Encrypt data at rest to ensure it is tamper-proof.

Regular monitoring and testing

In either case, you will need to sit down and seriously consider how your PCI compliance will be maintained. This is no easy task, as PCI necessitates ongoing monitoring of the network activity to validate that processes and policies for security, change and access management, and user validation are in place and up to date.

The trick to an operational and successful management system is its risk management, logging, auditing and monitoring. These basic functions will ensure ongoing compliance, by providing a management system designed to take live feeds from all three functions.

The testing of all these basic requirements should be laid down in a document, this could be a simple table (similar to Figure 11 – Validation action table, but could include some of the monitoring, review, audit and testing cycles required).

Figure 13 – Examples of testing schedule (levels are based on defined volume and/or PCI requirements)

Test Number	Validation action	Validation by	Occurrence
1	On-site PCI data security assessment	Qualified Security Assessor or Internal Auditor if signed by officer of the entity	Annually or quarterly
2	Annual PCI self-assessment questionnaire	Audit if signed by officer of the entity and Internal Audit Team	Annually
3	Quarterly network scan	ASV or part of internal PEN Test Team	Quarterly
4	Test change management back out procedures	Internal Security Team	Annually
5	Test problem and incident management procedures	Internal Security Team	Annually
6	Auditing schedules	Internal Audit Team	Monthly
7	Review risk register	Internal Security Team	Monthly

8	Review set of defined logs	Internal Security Team	Weekly
9	Monitor network, IDS, IPS	Internal Security Team	Daily
10	Test BCM and DR plans	Internal Audit Team	Quarterly

The net effect is that you should have a management system that closely aligns with Figure 14. Of course, each implementation will change from where and when key inputs and outputs are taken, but the essence should be the same.

Figure 14 – PCI compliant information security management system (ISMS)

Arriving where you want to be: PCI compliant

The previous tables make it clear that most of the challenge in implementing PCI lies in the technical and administrative aspects of the Standard. This is not surprising, given that most of the risk to cardholder data arises from exploits that target technical and administrative weaknesses in procedural and operational based security.

The fact that PCI requires ongoing validation of security efforts, coupled with the fact that security exploits are constantly changing, makes it clear that your entity cannot implement 'install and forget' solutions.

Even the best security efforts will fail occasionally. However, this is often made worse if they are not co-ordinated and integrated within the overall business processes/model, and can ensure that people or departments within the entity are not changing security safeguards or avoiding difficult policies and/or procedures.

You need to be prepared to back up your PCI validation efforts with records that can demonstrate compliance (i.e. evidence of audit findings and log management info). In addition, PCI contains numerous requirements for logging, tracking and the ability to present auditable records. This includes measures that will detect whether, how and when unauthorised changes are made to systems or records.

Section 10.5.5 of PCI requires the use of 'file integrity monitoring/change detection software on logs to ensure that existing log data cannot be changed without generating alerts'. In other words, when the third party, independent assessors who have been certified by the credit card entity drop by to perform the annual on-site audit, entities must be prepared to produce clear, comprehensive and reliable records demonstrating compliance.

Demonstrating compliance – ROC

PCI compliance also provides details on the expected content that should form part of the annual submission report – the 'report on compliance' (ROC) or 'executive summary report'.

Instructions and content for report on compliance

The ROC document should be used by auditors as the template for creating the report on compliance. The audited entity should follow each payment card entity's respective reporting requirements to ensure each payment card entity acknowledges the entity's compliance status. Contact with each payment card entity to determine each entity's reporting requirements and instructions is well worth the effort.

All assessors must follow the instructions for report content and format when completing a report on compliance:

Contact information and report date

- Include contact information for merchant or service provider and assessor.
- Date of report.

Executive summary

Include the following:

- Business description.
- List service providers and other entities with which the entity shares cardholder data.
- List processor relationships.
- Describe whether entity is directly connected to payment card entity.
- For merchants, POS products used.
- Any wholly-owned entities that require compliance with the PCI DSS.

- Any international entities that require compliance with the PCI DSS.
- Any wireless LANs and/or wireless POS terminals connected to the cardholder environment.

Description of scope of work and approach taken

- Version of the security audit procedures document used to conduct the assessment.
- Time-frame of assessment.
- Environment on which assessment focused (for example, entity's Internet access points, internal corporate network, processing points for the payment card entity).
- Any areas excluded from the review.
- Brief description or high-level drawing of network topology and controls.
- List of individuals interviewed.
- List of documentation reviewed.

Maintaining your PCI compliance

The following sections have been provided to help you maintain your compliance with the PCI Standard. The sections are, in effect, mapping examples that will help you remain compliant to PCI DSS, by creating a table which can be measured, monitored and reported against. I have found this a considerably easier way to track what is required for each area of PCI scope. For simplicity, I have broken this down into the three minimum areas of compliance (which yet cause maximum problems):

1 Example compliance mapping for the current environment – this looks holistically across all the areas of scope.
2 Example compliance mapping for the 'application' environment – clearly this depends on your web application, but nonetheless, a useful tool to help comply and drive results from your third party vendors.
3 Example compliance mapping for the POS environment – again a difficult area to demonstrate, so hopefully this will help focus your compliance efforts.

Example compliance mapping for your current environment

The example compliance mapping will help you remain compliant to PCI DSS. It details the processes that will need to be completed regularly to maintain PCI DSS compliance across all scope areas and applications. Use this to ensure your overall compliance programme is operational and effective.

The key:

- **PCI control #** references the control number within the PCI Standard associated with the activity.
- **Frequency** indicates how often the activity is performed.
- **Action** indicates the general area and action required by the Actor.
- **Owner** indicates who will be performing the action.
- **Description** provides supplementary information for the activity.

#	PCI Control #	Frequency	Action	Owner	Description
1.	Scoping	Quarterly, or upon significant changes to the network	**Update and maintain the PCI in-scope asset inventory**	IT Security Leader	The Information Security Team updates the PCI in-scope asset inventory, which includes hostnames, IP addresses, and owners. The inventory contains systems which store, process, or transmit cardholder data. It also contains infrastructure supporting the PCI environment, including Domain Controllers and virtual image hosts. Finally, the list contains other systems within a PCI secure zone and the DMZ, such as the front end [Application]. The inventory is critical to ensure that all security processes, such as vulnerability scanning or log collection, apply to the appropriate scope of systems. Any changes to current systems or the addition or decommissioning of systems applicable to PCI must be reflected in the list.
2.	All	Annually	Certify PCI compliance annually	IT Security Leader	The Information Security Team will certify the [Entity's] PCI compliance annually.

#	PCI Control #	Frequency	Action	Owner	Description
3.	1.1	Every six months and upon changes to firewall rules	**Review firewall rule sets and approve any changes**	IT Security Leader, Network Services Leader	Firewalls filtering connections into and out of the cardholder data environment, including the DMZ and the PCI secure zone, must have the full firewall rule set reviewed to determine if business justifications are still valid for each. This review should be documented. Changes are logged in the change management database. Any changes to the firewall rule set are approved by the Information Security Team to ensure that they do not conflict with the [Entity] security or PCI requirements (e.g. allows telnet).
4.	1.2	Ongoing	**Validate firewall rules**	Network Team	The NetworkTeam will review firewall rules at least every six months and may occasionally approach the application teams to validate rules that apply to their application.

#	PCI Control #	Frequency	Action	Owner	Description
5.	3.6.4	Annually, or upon suspected or actual breach, or if a key custodian leaves the company	**Rotate encryption keys for the [Application] and POS applications**	IT Security Leader	Encryption keys must be rotated at least annually, or in the case of a suspected or actual breach, or if a key custodian leaves the entity. The POS PA-DSS application has built-in functionality to rotate the keys, but this facility must be executed manually. The PA-DSS documentation outlines this procedure[42]. The POS Team has a process in place to rotate the keys. Information Security alerts the POS team 60 days in advance of the required deadline to initiate the key rotation process. The Information Security Team also validates with the POS Team that the key rotation has occurred. On last publication of this document, the key must be rotated before August 1 each year. The [Application] Team has developed a utility which allows for key rotation. Two custodians are required to input their half of the key, which they save in a secure location, to create a new key for the [Application] database. The Information Security Team co-ordinates with the Key Custodians (the CIO and PCI Data Owner at last publication) and the [Application] Team to initiate the key rotation process as outlined in the [Application] key rotation document[43] and validate its completion. On last publication of this document, the key must be rotated before June 1 each year.

[42] Please see the POS PA-DSS Implementation Guide in the PCI Relevant Documents section - *www.pcisecuritystandards.org/security_standards/documents.php.*
[43] Please see the [Application] Key Rotation document in the PCI Relevant Documents section - *www.pcisecuritystandards.org/security_standards/documents.php.*

#	PCI Control #	Frequency	Action	Owner	Description
6.	10.6	Ongoing	**Support security log review** – The teams will respond to Information Security requests based on alerts, as needed	IT Director; Online Retail Director	Security logs, including OS, DB and applications logs that are sent to [Logging Application], will be reviewed daily by the [Entity] Information Security Team. The Information Security Team will conduct an initial triage. If additional help is needed, the Information Security Team may request assistance from the appropriate leader. The Information Security Team or the Incident Response Team will alert the appropriate owner of detected suspicious activity, applicable to the [Entity] environment and the owner's responsibilities. This activity is derived from alerts generated from monitoring tools (e.g. File Integrity Monitoring – FIM, vulnerability scanning) and other security monitoring processes to detect suspicious activity, open vulnerabilities, unauthorised access, etc. For activity deemed a potential critical incident, as defined by the Incident Response Standard, the owner will need to acknowledge and begin to investigate the incident within 4 hours. For all other activity, the owner will need to acknowledge and begin to investigate the incident within 24 hours.

#	PCI Control #	Frequency	Action	Owner	Description
7.	6.3 6.3.1 - 6.3.7	Ongoing	**Validate, schedule and test patches** – The teams will validate, schedule and participate in the testing of critical security application and operating system patches, as needed	IT Director; Online Retail Director	Critical application and operating system security patches must be tested and installed within 30 days of notification from the [Entity] Information Security Team or vendor. The teams will work closely with the vendors, so that the application and system remains up to date on vendor security patches, if any. The Directors/VP will be responsible for the scheduling and testing of patches.

#	PCI Control #	Frequency	Action	Owner	Description
8.	6.4	Per code release and/or change event	**Change control process** –The [Application] Application Team will follow [Entity]'s Change Management Policy, as needed. All custom code will be reviewed and Release Engineers rather than developers will push new code into production	IT Director	All changes to production must be tested and follow [Entity]'s change management process. The [Application] Team will follow the formal change control process in which Release Engineers rather than developers push new code into production. Developers will not have access to production.

The [Application] Team must ensure code is reviewed for security vulnerabilities. Any findings must be remediated prior to releasing to production. Vulnerabilities must be documented and signed off by management. |

#	PCI Control #	Frequency	Action	Owner	Description
9.	6.4 6.4.1 - 6.4.4	Ongoing	**Follow change management policy** – The teams will follow [Entity]'s Change Management Policy, as needed	IT Director; Online Retail Director; Internal Audit	All software modifications and operating system configuration changes to production must be tested and follow [Entity]'s change management process.
10	6.5	Ongoing and upon new hire	**OWASP training** – The [Application] development team will be trained in OWASP secure coding techniques	IT Director; Director of Apps Development	All members of the [Application] Development Team, including new hires, will be trained in OWASP secure coding techniques.

#	PCI Control #	Frequency	Action	Owner	Description
11	6.4, 6.4.1 - 6.4.4	Weekly	**Ensure security is part of the software development lifecycle through the change management process**	IT Security Leader	Changes to applications can open or create security holes. The Information Security Team must analyse changes to the in-scope environment and applications to ensure security is considered. For example, changes with impact to separation of duties, new or different uses of PANs, testing, access control and monitoring should be reviewed for adherence to [Entity] policies and PCI requirements. Non-compliant, or insecure, changes should be remediated before going live in production.

#	PCI Control #	Frequency	Action	Owner	Description
12	6.3, 6.3.1 - 6.3.7	Monthly	**Identify system components requiring security patches**	IT Security Leader	Information Security identifies system components which are missing critical security patches and will alert infrastructure owners to patch those components via [Request Management Application]. Information Security uses vulnerability scanning and security or vendor bulletins to stay abreast of critical security patches which apply to the [Entity] environment. The patch management process[44] must then be followed to alert on and apply patches. Infrastructure and Application Teams are required to test and patch their systems within 30 days of notification. However, if testing and change management schedules are initiated upon notification and unnecessary pauses in the deployment of patches are omitted, a longer application cycle may be permitted.

---

[44] Please see the Patch Management and Vulnerability Scanning process documents in the PCI Relevant Documents section.

#	PCI Control #	Frequency	Action	Owner	Description
13	3.6.3, 3.6.4	Annually	**Encryption key rotation** – The [Application] Application Team will be responsible for rotating the encryption keys annually	IT Director; Online Retail Director	Encryption keys must be rotated annually. The [Entity] Information Security Team will initiate the process, while the [Application] Team supports the use of the Java Encryption Utility to input and swap the keys. POS encryption keys must be rotated annually according to the POS PA-DSS Implementation Guide.

#	PCI Control #	Frequency	Action	Owner	Description
14	3.6.3, 3.6.4	Annually	**Validate integrity of encryption key** – The Server administrator will check the data integrity of the Key Encryption Key residing on the USB keys	Server Administrator Team	Encryption keys for the [Application] application cannot be rotated annually. Compensating controls are in place for the secure storage of the key. The [Application] administrator will check the data integrity of the Key Encryption Key residing on the USB keys[45].

---

[45] Please see Compensating Control document in the PCI Relevant Documents section - *www.pcisecuritystandards.org/security_standards/documents.php.*

#	PCI Control #	Frequency	Action	Owner	Description
15	2.2, 6.2	Annually	**Maintain and update the platform secure configuration standards**	IT Security Leader	Each operating system, middleware, and database platform which comprise the PCI in-scope environment, have an approved secure configuration standard based on industry accepted practices. These standards are divided into a Tier 1 group (currently configured) and a Tier 2 group (not currently configured). The Tier 2 controls either are not applicable for [Entity]'s environment, or the level of effort is disproportionate to the risk and other mitigating controls are in place. As threats and risks to the environment change, as well as updates to industry practices are announced, Information Security should update the Standards accordingly and ensure they are applied. Information from vulnerability scans or from the Center for Information Security are sources for such potential updates. Additionally, Tier 2 items should be reassessed for applicability and risk to determine if they should be migrated to Tier 1.

#	PCI Control #	Frequency	Action	Owner	Description
16	2.2, 6.2	Ongoing	**Schedule and test secure configuration standards –** The teams will schedule and test changes to the secure configuration standards for their environments, as needed	IT Director; Internal Audit	Operating system and database secure configuration standards may be updated as new risks to the environment are identified or as industry standard practices change. Though Information Security and the IT Infrastructure Groups will deploy these changes, the appropriate Director/VP will need to support the appropriate change control and testing processes, as needed. The Standards will be updated regularly according to industry standards.

#	PCI Control #	Frequency	Action	Owner	Description
17	11.2	Quarterly	**Validate and remediate vulnerability scanning findings –** The teams will remediate, investigate and address internal and external vulnerability scanning findings before the next scheduled scan, as needed	IT Director	The [Entity] Information Security Team will conduct internal vulnerability scans quarterly while a third party accredited vendor, Accuvant, will perform separate external vulnerability scans quarterly. Any findings requiring action will be shared with the appropriate team; the appropriate Directors / Senior Management Team will address the findings or support remediation activity, through scheduling and testing, before the next quarterly vulnerability scan. Critical internal findings (CVSS 2.0 score of 7.0 or higher) and above-medium external findings (CVSS 2.0 score of 4.0 or higher) from the vulnerability scans will need to be remediated.

#	PCI Control #	Frequency	Action	Owner	Description
18	11.2	Quarterly	**Perform vulnerability scanning**	IT Security Leader	Information Security performs quarterly scans, currently with a [Vulnerability scanning application] scanner with up-to-date plug-ins, of all system components which comprise the cardholder data environment quarterly. The vulnerability scanning process[46] must then be followed to alert on and remediate discovered vulnerabilities. At least, critical vulnerabilities must be alerted on and remediated. False positives are marked as such, so that the next scan will not alert on them. Vulnerabilities identified in one scan should not reappear in the next quarter's scan.

---

[46] Please see the Vulnerability Scanning process document in the PCI Relevant Documents section - *www.pcisecuritystandards.org/security_standards/documents.php.*

#	PCI Control #	Frequency	Action	Owner	Description
19	11.3	Annually	**Co-ordinate penetration testing**	IT Security Leader	Annually, a penetration test is performed on the cardholder data environment. A third party with security penetration testing expertise can perform this exercise. The test should target network and application layer vulnerabilities. Penetration testing often has similar impact and remediation follows the same processes as vulnerability scanning.

#	PCI Control #	Frequency	Action	Owner	Description
20	11.3	Annually	**Validate and remediate penetration testing findings –** The teams will investigate penetration testing findings and remediate before the next scheduled scan, as needed	IT Director; Online Retail Director	The [Entity] Information Security Team will schedule and conduct (or a third party will conduct) penetration testing annually. The Directors/VP will be notified of scheduling ahead of time. The Information Security Team or the Incident Response Team will alert the appropriate owner of detected suspicious activity, applicable to the [Entity] environment and the owner's responsibilities. This activity is derived from alerts generated from monitoring tools (e.g. FIM, vulnerability scanning) and other security monitoring processes to detect suspicious activity, open vulnerabilities, unauthorised access. For activity deemed a potential critical incident, as defined by the Incident Response Standard, the owner will need to acknowledge and begin to investigate the incident within 4 hours. For all other activity, the owner will need to acknowledge and begin to investigate the incident within 24 hours.

#	PCI Control #	Frequency	Action	Owner	Description
21	12.1	Annually	**Maintain programme sustainability**	IT Security Leader	Until a formal governance or compliance team is assigned full responsibility, the Information Security Team will have the interim responsibility, in conjunction with the PCI Data Owner, to validate the PCI Programme is on track to ensure [Entity]'s continued compliance. This includes ensuring sustainable processes are being executed by the responsible parties and that appropriate evidence of such exists. Also, Information Security will identify changes to the environment (i.e. a new payment application) which may impact scope and conduct an assessment to apply the appropriate controls to the new scope. Finally, periodic validation of compliance is assessed. A qualified third party can assist [Entity] in these activities.

#	PCI Control #	Frequency	Action	Owner	Description
22	12.1.2	Annually	**Conduct annual risk assessment**	IT Security Leader	The Risk Assessment Policy [47] outlines a risk management framework, based on ISO27001 and ISO27005, which enable Information Security to conduct periodic risk assessment and aligns activity to the ISO Plan-Do-Check-Act model. An approach is outlined for risk identification, estimation, and evaluation, as well as post assessment activity, such as risk treatment and risk acceptance. The Information Security Team conducts a risk assessment of the cardholder data environment annually. Processes, documentations, standards, and controls must be modified, if required, such that the risks to the environment are minimised to an acceptable level.

---

[47] Please see the Risk Assessment policy document in the PCI Relevant Documents section.

#	PCI Control #	Frequency	Action	Owner	Description
23	12.8	Annually	**Manage third party security and agreements**	IT Security Leader	The Information Security Team must validate that third parties which are considered service providers related to [Entity]'s cardholder data (e.g. cardholder data is shared with them) are PCI compliant annually. The third party should produce documentation, which [Entity] keeps on file, showing compliance. Payment applications deployed within the [Entity's] environment must be validated on the PCI SSC's website for continued PA-DSS certification for the version installed. If a version is no longer certified as PA-DSS compliant, the [Entity] must upgrade to a version, or alternate software, that is PA-DSS compliant.

#	PCI Control #	Frequency	Action	Owner	Description
24	12.9	Annually	**Maintain the incident response programme**	IT Security Leader	The Information Security Team maintains the Incident Response Plan[48] and Programme, including staffing the Computer Incident Response Team (CIRT), ensuring personnel are available 24x7 to respond to alerts, and conducting annual testing of the Incident Response Plan. Results from vulnerability scanning, monitoring activities, risk assessments, and changes to the environment may impact and require changes to the Incident Response Plan. The annual testing simulates an incident with key stakeholders, including the CIRT, to ensure roles and responsibilities are understood.

---

[48] Please see CSIRTs - *www.cert.org/csirts/*.

#	PCI Control #	Frequency	Action	Owner	Description
25	3.1, 4.2, 6.3.4, 11.1-11.5	Quarterly	**Execute the DLP processes**	IT Security Leader	The Information Security Team must follow [Entity]'s DLP Processes[49] using [DLP scanning tool], the DLP scanning tool, to identify rogue caches of cardholder data. This may include scans of e-mail boxes, file shares, and databases. Though a sample of each potential area can be scanned per quarter, ideally all potential file shares, databases, and e-mail inboxes are scanned over the course of a year.
					Test systems are scanned for the use of production data. Manual validation of data used in the POS and [Application] test system are required. The Information Security Team compares a sample of data used in test to a list of approved test data (as provided by an acquiring bank for test purposes).

[49] Please see the Data Loss Prevention document in the PCI Relevant Documents section.

#	PCI Control #	Frequency	Action	Owner	Description
26	6.3.1.5, 7.1, 7.2	Ongoing	**Follow ARF process for changes in access controls –** The teams will follow the ARF process for any Hire, Term and Change access requests	[Entity] Director; [Entity] Director; Retail, [Entity] Director; [Entity] VP, [Entity] Lead	Changes in access, including additions, terminations, or modifications, must follow the ARF process.

#	PCI Control #	Frequency	Action	Owner	Description
27	6.3.1.5, 7.1, 7.2	Every six months	**Perform user recertification**	IT Security Leader	All users and administrators with access to system components within the cardholder data environment are reviewed to ensure they still are required to have the access assigned to them. Currently, Information Security collects the list of accounts and requests a review, via e-mail, from the application owners. The application owners respond either by accepting that all users have access required to perform their job function, or indicate where access changes are required to align with job functions. Changes are implemented through the ARF process. Going forward, automated tools to track access and receive periodic approval are being considered.

#	PCI Control #	Frequency	Action	Owner	Description
28	6.3.1.5, 7.1, 7.2	Ongoing	**Review vendor access rights** – The team will complete any changes to vendor access through the a defined process for access to the [Application]	IT Director, Online Retail Director	All changes to vendor access and accounts (user maintenance, configuration, etc.) will undergo a review process. Changes will be completed on the [External access application]. These changes will occur on the [External access application] by the IT Infrastructure team, such that vendors only access the [Entity] environment through the [Application].

#	PCI Control #	Frequency	Action	Owner	Description
29	6.3.1.5, 7.1, 7.2	Ongoing	**Review vendor access rights for POS** – The POS Application Team will complete any changes to vendor access through a defined process for allowing access via the Application]	POS Application Team; Infrastructure and Operations Team	All access to the POS registers and servers will occur through the [External access application].

#	PCI Control #	Frequency	Action	Owner	Description
30	6.3.1.5, 7.1, 7.2	Bi-annual	**Validate access controls** – The teams will validate access to their respective systems bi-annually	IT Director, Online Retail Director	The Directors/VP will validate all access to their systems at least bi-annually for his/her team (other business units will validate their own users). The Information Security Team will initiate requests to the team leads to acknowledge that users who have access, including privileged users, have a business justification for that access. Access controls will be reviewed regularly by the [Entity] Information Security Team.

#	PCI Control #	Frequency	Action	Owner	Description
31	10.6, 12.2	Daily	**Conduct daily log reviews and alert response**	IT Security Leader	Logs and audit trails are collected and reviewed by [Entity] centrally using [Logging Application]. Which logs and audit trails are available for review within [Logging Application] are a function of the logging enabled on a particular system component and if that system component is configured to send those logs to [Logging Application], either via a push (i.e. syslog or [Logging Application] forwarder agent) or a pull (i.e. [Logging Application] 'app' collector). All system components in the cardholder data environment send logs to [Logging Application]. This includes audit trails in operating systems, databases and middleware logging facilities. Also included in [Logging Application] logs are wireless rogue device detection alerts, intrusion detection system logs, antivirus logs, file integrity monitoring logs and application logs.

[Logging Application] includes capabilities to ensure integrity of received logs and logs are stored for at least one year. [Logging Application] contains several preconfigured reports; some reports are focused on PCI, such as shared account access, and allows for specific alerting based on custom-defined rules and thresholds.

Information security reviews logs at least daily for generic access attempts, access escalation, configuration changes, unauthorised access to cardholder data, and other potentially anomalous behaviour. This daily review will be facilitated by automated correlation rules. In the event of an incident, the incident response process is executed to perform proper triage, escalation, containment, and remediation. |

#	PCI Control #	Frequency	Action	Owner	Description
32	10.6, 12.5.2	Ongoing	**Enhance rule-driven automated alerts**	IT Security Leader	Security event incident management is an ongoing, continuously evolving and maturing process. As the Information Security Team better understands the environment, the impact of changes and overall risks, the monitoring capabilities will improve. One focus area for Information Security is defining additional rules to generate automated alerts. Apart from out-of-the-box functionality and reporting, custom alerts will allow for more timely and granular insight into activity in the cardholder data environment, increasing the Information Security Team's abilities at detecting and preventing malicious behaviour. Areas for additional alerts include appropriate access to cardholder data aligned to business rules, administrative actions and changes to system level objects.
33	6.3.1.5, 7.1, 7.2, 8.5	Weekly, or as needed	**Participate in access request form (ARF) approvals**	IT Security Leader	Access requests for system components which comprise the cardholder data environment are approved by Information Security. The Information Security Team limits access to only those individuals whose job requires such access.

#	PCI Control #	Frequency	Action	Owner	Description
34	6.3.1.5, 7.1, 7.2, 8.5	Weekly, or as needed	**Validate terminated users are removed**	IT Security Leader	Upon notification from HR or otherwise, Information Security ensures the Infrastructure and Application Teams remove a terminated user's access from system components which comprise the cardholder data environment.
35	12.6, 12.1.1, 12.1.2	Annually	**Complete PCI awareness training** – All associates that handle ChD will undergo annual PCI awareness training	POS, Application Teams, Infrastructure Team, Business Operations Team	All team members with access to cardholder data or privileged access to applications and in-scope infrastructure must complete an annual PCI awareness training course designed, deployed, and managed by the Information Security Team. Part of the training will require acknowledgement of [Entity]'s Information Security Policies. This is web-based training. Associates will receive an annual reminder.

#	PCI Control #	Frequency	Action	Owner	Description
36	12.6, 12.1.1, 12.1.2	Annually	**Operate security awareness programme**	IT Security Leader	All individuals, including those with access to cardholder data, privileged access to systems in scope for PCI, and executives must participate in the awareness programme.
					The programme involves disseminating information using two media. For store associates, the media are a training course taught by the store leads and an End-user Policy[50] containing the applicable policies. For home office and call centre, the media are web-based training and posters hung in break rooms.
					The Information Security Team ensures that the training is scheduled and conducted annually. The Information Security Team also owns the content, which can be updated, enhanced, or modified to reflect changes in focus, but should always reflect the importance in protecting cardholder data.
					In all cases, recipients of the training must acknowledge in writing that they have read and understood [Entity]'s Security Awareness and Acceptable Use Policy. This should be done and collected at time of annual training. The Information Security Team must ensure these are properly collected for store training. CBT's are automatically catalogued in the Learning Management System.

#	PCI Control #	Frequency	Action	Owner	Description
37	12.6, 12.1.1, 12.1.2	Annually	**Review and update policies and procedures applicable to PCI compliance**	IT Security Leader	All policies, including the Security Awareness and Acceptable Use Policy, must be reviewed for applicability at least annually. The appropriate owner, stakeholders, and Information Security Team, update the documents and review date based on changes to the environment, if any, and publish the changes following [Entity]'s Documentation Change Control Policies[51].

---

[50] Please see the End User Policy examples at *www.sans.org/security-resources/policies/computer.php*.

[51] Please see Change Control at *www.sans.org/security-resources/policies/computer.php*.

#	PCI Control #	Frequency	Action	Owner	Description
38	11.5	Ongoing	**Validate and remediate any file integrity monitoring (FIM) findings** - The teams will respond to any FIM alerts, as needed	IT Director	File integrity monitoring alerts will be reviewed by the [Entity] Information Security Team. The Information Security Team or the Incident Response Team will alert the appropriate owner of detected suspicious activity, applicable to the [Entity] environment and the owner's responsibilities. This activity is derived from alerts generated from monitoring tools (e.g. FIM, vulnerability scanning,) and other security monitoring processes to detect suspicious activity, open vulnerabilities, unauthorised access, etc. For activity deemed a potential critical incident, as defined by the Incident Response Standard, the owner will need to acknowledge and begin to investigate the incident within 4 hours. For all other activity, the owner will need to acknowledge and begin to investigate the incident within 24 hours. Any additional files to be monitored will be communicated to the Information Security Team by the Directors/VP.

#	PCI Control #	Frequency	Action	Owner	Description
39	3.1, 9.7, 12.1.1, 12.1.2, 12.6	Ongoing, but a validation is required at least quarterly	**Support the PCI data owner and data classification policy**	IT Security Leader	The Data Classification Policy details a PCI Data Owner with the responsibility of safeguarding PCI-relevant information within the [Entity] environment. The Data Classification Policy also declares required security standards for PCI-relevant data. The Information Security Team's primary role, as outlined in the Data Classification Policy, is to provide technical advice on information technology security to Data Owners and the Data Protection Council (not yet formalised). As changes to the standards and policy arise, for example by new threats or uses of data, Information Security should co-ordinate with data owners and administrators to understand the impact of those changes to the business and advise in the deployment of those changes. Further, Information Security incorporates training materials related to the data classification and standards for inclusion in the [Entity] Awareness Programme, such as in new hire and periodic training.

#	PCI Control #	Frequency	Action	Owner	Description
40	4.2	Ongoing	**Securely Transfer ChD** – All transmissions of ChD must be done securely	Business Operations Team	The Business Operations Team will consult the Information Security Team when transmitting ChD to third parties for the first time. If an existing regular transmission schedule is followed, the [Entity] Lead will ensure the ChD is being securely transmitted.

Future PCI compliance considerations

The discipline of fully evaluating new processes, applications, or significant changes to the environment is beyond the scope of this book. However, the following are considerations as entities' payment environments grow:

- Will new processes/applications store, process, or transmit cardholder data?
  - o If the answer is no, then the process and application is out of scope for PCI.
  - o If the answer is yes, is it absolutely necessary that the process/application does so with the full PAN?
    - o If the answer is no, then a decision must be made weighing the costs (compliance, security risk, etc.) vs. benefits (business functionality) of using full PAN.
    - o If full PAN is required (or it is determined that the benefit outweighs the cost/risk), then the application should be placed within the PCI zones to isolate the ChD and, therefore, maintain a minimal scope.
- If a payment application is a part of the settlement or authorisation process, then the application should be certified PA-DSS compliant.
  - o Most payment software applications will provide an Implementation or Best Practice Guide with steps to configure the application to be PA-DSS compliant that when followed, reduces the PCI compliance burden for entity.
  - o The infrastructure will need the full breadth of requirements, but the application can follow the

Implementation Guide or Best Practice Guide provided by the vendor.

o   This also applies to upgrades, as each *version* of an application must be certified.

o   Do not implement a payment application that is not certified PA-DSS.

- Entities Security Risk Assessment methodology and processes should be used to evaluate the risks associated with bringing the application online.
- The new application or process should be evaluated against the latest version of the PCI DSS. The security processes applied to other application areas and designed to be scalable will likely need to be applied to the new or changed infrastructure and will contribute significantly to meeting many of the PCI requirements.
- Will there be third parties involved? If so, please see the section Third Party Considerations.
- PCI required documentation will need to be updated (e.g. ChD flows, inventories).
- If the application or process is not PA-DSS (i.e. not a payment application), non-standard, or otherwise complex, outside third party subject matter experts can provide additional guidance to help [Entity] navigate the nuances of PCI compliance through the viewpoint of the Assessor community.

Example compliance mapping for applications

Example sustainability mapping for applications within your PCI environment is outlined in the table below.

The key:

- **PCI control #** references the control number within the PCI Standard associated with the activity.
- **Frequency** indicates how often the activity is performed.
- **Action** indicates the general area and action required by the Actor.
- **Owner** indicates who will be performing the action.
- **Description** provides supplementary information for the activity.
- **Other related process** maps the activity to other relevant activities within this document.

#	PCI Control #	Frequency	Action	Owner	Description
1	3.6.3, 3.6.4	Annually	**Validate integrity of encryption key** – The server administrator will check the data integrity of the key encryption key residing on the USB keys	Server Administrator Team	Encryption keys cannot be rotated annually. Compensating controls are in place for the secure storage of the key. The [Application] administrator will check the data integrity of the Key Encryption Key residing on the USB keys[52] .

---

[52] Please see *www.pcisecuritystandards.org/pdfs/pci_audit_procedures_v1-1.pdf*.

#	PCI Control #	Frequency	Action	Owner	Description
2	11.3	Annually	**Validate and remediate penetration testing findings –** The [Application] Application Team will remediate, investigate and address penetration testing findings before the next scheduled scan, as needed	IT Director	The [Entity] Information Security Team will schedule and conduct (or a third party will conduct) penetration testing annually. The [Entity] Director will be notified of scheduling ahead of time. The Information Security Team or the Incident Response Team will alert the [Entity] Director of detected suspicious activity, applicable to the [Application] environment and the [Entity] Director's responsibilities. This activity is derived from alerts generated from monitoring tools (e.g. FIM, vulnerability scanning) and other security monitoring processes to detect suspicious activity, open vulnerabilities, unauthorised access, etc. For activity deemed a potential critical incident, as defined by the Incident Response Standard, the [Entity] Director will need to acknowledge and begin to investigate the incident within 4 hours. For all other activity, the [Entity] Director will need to acknowledge and begin to investigate the incident within 24 hours.

#	PCI Control #	Frequency	Action	Owner	Description
3	12.6, 12.1.1, 12.1.2	Annually	**Complete PCI awareness training** – All associates that handle ChD will undergo annual PCI awareness training	Application Team	All [Application] Team members with access to cardholder data or privileged access to [Application] applications and in-scope infrastructure must complete annual PCI awareness training course designed, deployed, and managed by the Information Security Team. Part of the training will require acknowledgement of [Entity]'s Information Security Policies. This is web-based training. Associates will receive an annual reminder.
4	6.3.1.5, 7.1, 7.2	Bi-annually	**Validate access controls** – The [Application] Application Team will validate access to [Application] systems bi-annually	IT Director	The [Entity] IT Director will validate all access to the [Application] systems at least bi-annually for his/her team (other business units will validate their own users). The Information Security Team will initiate requests to the [Application] Team Leads to acknowledge that users who have access, including privileged users, have a business justification for that access. Access controls will be reviewed regularly by the [Entity] Information Security Team.

#	PCI Control #	Frequency	Action	Owner	Description
5	10.6	Ongoing	**Support security log review** – The Application Team will respond to information security requests based on alerts, as needed	IT Director	Security logs, including OS, DB and applications logs that are sent to [Logging Application], will be reviewed daily by the [Entity] Information Security Team. The Information Security Team will conduct an initial triage; if additional help is needed, the Information Security Team may request assistance from the [Entity] IT Director. The Information Security Team, or the Incident Response Team, will alert the [Entity] IT Director of detected suspicious activity, applicable to the [Application] environment and the [Entity] Director's responsibilities. This activity is derived from alerts generated from monitoring tools (e.g. FIM, vulnerability scanning) and other security monitoring processes to detect suspicious activity, open vulnerabilities, unauthorised access, etc.

#	PCI Control #	Frequency	Action	Owner	Description
6	6.3, 6.3.1 - 6.3.7	Ongoing	**Validate, schedule and test patches** – The [Application] Application Team will validate, schedule and participate in the testing of critical security application and operating system patches, as needed	IT Director	Critical application and operating system security patches must be tested and installed within 30 days of notification from the [Entity] Information Security Team or vendor. The [Application] Application Team will work closely with the [Application] vendors, so that the application remains up to date on vendor security patches, if any. The [Entity] IT Director will be responsible for the scheduling and testing of patches.

#	PCI Control #	Frequency	Action	Owner	Description
7	6.4, 6.4.1 - 6.4.4	Ongoing	**Follow change management policy** – The [Application] Application Team will follow [Entity]'s change management policy, as needed	IT Director	All software modifications and operating system configuration changes to production must be tested and follow [Entity]'s change management process.

#	PCI Control #	Frequency	Action	Owner	Description
8	2.2, 6.2	Ongoing	**Schedule and test secure configuration standards** – The [Application] Application Team will schedule and test changes to the secure configuration standards for the [Application] environment, as needed	IT Director	[Application] operating system and database secure configuration standards may be updated as new risks to the environment are identified, or as industry standard practices change. Though Information Security and the IT Infrastructure Groups will deploy these changes, the [Entity] IT Director will need to support the appropriate change control and testing processes as needed. The Standards will be updated regularly according to industry standards.

#	PCI Control #	Frequency	Action	Owner	Description
9	6.3.1.5, 7.1, 7.2	Ongoing	**Utilise [External access application] for vendor access** – The Application Team will complete any changes to vendor access through the appropriate process for access to the Application	IT Director	All changes to vendor access and accounts (user maintenance, configuration, etc.) will undergo the appropriate process. Changes will be completed on the [External access application]. These changes will occur on the [External access application] by the IT Infrastructure team such that vendors only access via the prescribed method.

#	PCI Control #	Frequency	Action	Owner	Description
10	6.3.1.5, 7.1, 7.2	Ongoing	**Follow appropriate process for changes in access controls –** The Application Team will follow the appropriate process for any hire, term and change access requests	IT Director	Changes in access, including additions, terminations, or modifications, must follow the appropriate process.

#	PCI Control #	Frequency	Action	Owner	Description
11	11.5	Ongoing	**Validate and remediate any file integrity monitoring (FIM) findings** – The [Application] Application Team will respond to any FIM alerts, as needed.	IT Director	File Integrity Monitoring alerts will be reviewed by the [Entity] Information Security Team. The Information Security Team, or the Incident Response Team, will alert the [Entity] Director of detected suspicious activity, applicable to the [Application] environment and the [Entity] Director's responsibilities. This activity is derived from alerts generated from monitoring tools (e.g. FIM, vulnerability scanning) and other security monitoring processes to detect suspicious activity, open vulnerabilities, unauthorised access, etc. For activity deemed a potential critical incident, as defined by the Incident Response Standard, the [Entity] Director will need to acknowledge and begin to investigate the incident within 4 hours. For all other activity, the [Entity] Director will need to acknowledge and begin to investigate the incident within 24 hours. Any additional files to be monitored will be communicated to the Information Security Team by the [Entity] Director.

#	PCI Control #	Frequency	Action	Owner	Description
12	11.2	Quarterly	**Validate and remediate vulnerability scanning findings** –The Application Team will remediate, investigate and address internal and external vulnerability scanning findings before the next scheduled scan, as needed	IT Director	The [Entity] Information Security Team will conduct internal vulnerability scans quarterly while a third party accredited vendor, Accuvant, will perform separate external vulnerability scans quarterly. Any findings requiring action will be shared with the [Application] Team; the [Entity] Director will address the findings or support remediation activity, through scheduling and testing, before the next quarterly vulnerability scan. Critical internal findings (CVSS 2.0 score of 7.0 or higher)[53] and above-medium external findings (CVVS 2.0 score of 4.0 or higher) from the vulnerability scans will need to be remediated.

---

[53] See *www.first.org/cvss/cvss-guide.html.*

*Payment Application Data Security Standard (PA-DSS)
Application*

For the application layer, software that is PA-DSS certified
reduces the PCI compliance burden for the merchant, if
implemented under the software vendor's PA-DSS certified
configuration. Most payment software applications will
provide an implementation guide with steps to configure
the application to be PA-DSS compliant.

If the entity has configured their application layer according
to the vendor's implementation guide[54] to meet the
Payment Application Data Security Standard, and thus, PCI
compliance for that application, this configuration will need
to be maintained to ensure continued compliance.

PA-DSS applications must be recertified to ensure
continued compliance. If the entity's installed version
becomes no longer compliant, the application must be
upgraded to a version, or alternate software, that is. The
Information Security Team will monitor the compliance,
posted on the PCI SSC's website, annually and alert to
changes.

Application operating systems

PA-DSS, however, does not address the OS layer, and thus,
the responsibility remains on the merchant for compliance
at that layer. If the entity has implemented the following
control areas in the OS layer (i.e. iSeries, Windows®), then

---

[54] Please see PA-DSS Implementation Guide at
www.pcisecuritystandards.org/security_standards/documents.php

appropriate evidence of compliance must be maintained in the following:

- Hardening
- Access controls
- Logging and monitoring
- Antivirus.

Note: Antivirus is not always implemented on certain OS, because this particular OS is not commonly susceptible to viruses.

Example compliance mapping for POS

Compliance mapping for the POS environment is outlined in the table below. The table has the following description columns:

- **PCI control #** references the control number within the PCI Standard associated with the activity.
- **Frequency** indicates how often the activity is performed.
- **Action** indicates the general area and action required by the Actor.
- **Owner** indicates who will be performing the action.
- **Description** provides supplementary information for the activity.

#	PCI Control #	Frequency	Action	Owner	Description
1	3.6.3, 3.6.4	Annually	**Encryption key rotation** – The POS Application Team will be responsible for rotating the encryption keys annually	Retail, [Entity] Director	POS encryption keys must be rotated annually according to the POS PA-DSS Implementation Guide.

#	PCI Control #	Frequency	Action	Owner	Description
2	11.3	Annually	**Validate and remediate penetration testing findings** – The POS Application Team will remediate, investigate and address penetration testing findings before the next scheduled scan, as needed	Retail, IT Director	The [Entity] Information Security Team will schedule and conduct (or a third party will conduct) penetration testing annually. The Retail, [Entity] Director will be notified of scheduling ahead of time. The Information Security Team, or the Incident Response Team, will alert the Retail, [Entity] Director of detected suspicious activity, applicable to the POS environment and Retail, [Entity] Director's responsibilities. This activity is derived from alerts generated from monitoring tools (e.g. FIM, vulnerability scanning) and other security monitoring processes to detect suspicious activity, open vulnerabilities, unauthorised access, etc. For activity deemed a potential critical incident, as defined by the Incident Response Standard, the Retail, [Entity] Director will need to acknowledge and begin to investigate the incident within 4 hours. For all other activity, the Retail, [Entity] Director will need to acknowledge and begin to investigate the incident within 24 hours.

#	PCI Control #	Frequency	Action	Owner	Description
3	12.6, 12.1.1, 12.1.2	Annually	**Complete PCI awareness training** – All associates that handle ChD will undergo annual PCI awareness training	POS Application Team	All POS Team members with access to cardholder data or privileged access to POS applications and in-scope infrastructure must complete an annual PCI awareness training course designed, deployed, and managed by the Information Security team. Part of the training will require acknowledgement of [Entity]'s Information Security Policies. This is web-based training. Associates will receive an annual reminder.
4	6.3.1.5, 7.1, 7.2	Bi-annually	**Validate access controls** – The POS Application Team will validate access to POS systems bi-annually	Retail, IT Director	The Retail, IT Director will validate all access to the POS systems at least bi-annually for his/her team (other business units will validate their own users). The Information Security Team will initiate requests to the POS Team Leads to acknowledge that users who have access, including privileged users, have a business justification for that access. Access controls will be reviewed regularly by the [Entity] Information Security Team.

#	PCI Control #	Frequency	Action	Owner	Description
5	10.6	Ongoing	**Support security log review** – The POS Application Team will respond to information security requests based on alerts, as needed	Retail, IT Director	Security logs, including OS, DB and applications logs that are sent to [Logging Application], will be reviewed daily by the [Entity] Information Security Team. The Information Security Team will conduct an initial triage; if additional help is needed, the Information Security Team may request assistance from the Retail, [Entity] Director. The Information Security Team, or the Incident Response Team, will alert the Retail, [Entity] Director of detected suspicious activity, applicable to the POS environment and Retail, [Entity] Director's responsibilities. This activity is derived from alerts generated from monitoring tools (e.g. FIM, vulnerability scanning) and other security monitoring processes to detect suspicious activity, open vulnerabilities, unauthorised access, etc.

#	PCI Control #	Frequency	Action	Owner	Description
6	6.3, 6.3.1 - 6.3.7	Ongoing	**Validate, schedule and test patches –** The POS Application Team will validate, schedule and participate in the testing of critical security application and operating system patches, as needed	Retail, IT Director	Critical application and operating system security patches must be tested and installed within 30 days of notification from the [Entity] Information Security Team or vendor. The POS Application Team will work closely with the POS vendors, so that the application remains up to date on vendor security patches, if any.

The Retail, [Entity] Director will be responsible for the scheduling and testing of patches. |

#	PCI Control #	Frequency	Action	Owner	Description
7	6.4, 6.4.1 - 6.4.4	Ongoing	**Follow change management policy** – The POS Application Team will follow [Entity]'s change management policy, as needed	Retail, IT Director	All software modifications and operating system configuration changes to production must be tested and follow [Entity]'s change management process.

#	PCI Control #	Frequency	Action	Owner	Description
8	2.2, 6.2	Ongoing	**Schedule and test secure configuration standards** – The POS Application Team will schedule and test changes to the secure configuration standards for the POS environment, as needed	Retail, IT Director	POS operating system and database secure configuration standards may be updated as new risks to the environment are identified, or as industry standard practices change. Though Information Security and the IT Infrastructure Groups will deploy these changes, the Retail, [Entity] Director will need to support the appropriate change control and testing processes, as needed. The Standards will be updated regularly according to industry standards.

#	PCI Control #	Frequency	Action	Owner	Description
9	6.3.1.5, 7.1, 7.2	Ongoing	**Utilise [External access application] for vendor access** –The POS Application Team will complete any changes to vendor access through the ARF process for the [External access application]	Retail, IT Director	All changes to vendor access and accounts (user maintenance, configuration, etc.) will undergo the ARF process. Changes will be completed on the [External access application]. These changes will occur on the [External access application] by the IT Infrastructure Team, such that vendors only access POS through the [External access application]s.

#	PCI Control #	Frequency	Action	Owner	Description
10	6.3.1.5, 7.1, 7.2	Ongoing	**Utilise [External access application] for POS access –** The POS Application Team will complete any changes to vendor access through the ARF process for the [External access application]	POS Application Team	All access to the POS registers and servers will occur through the [External access application].

#	PCI Control #	Frequency	Action	Owner	Description
11	6.3.1.5, 7.1, 7.2	Ongoing	**Follow ARF process for changes in access controls** – The POS Application Team will follow the ARF process for any hire, term and change access requests	Retail, IT Director	Changes in access, including additions, terminations, or modifications, must follow the ARF process.

#	PCI Control #	Frequency	Action	Owner	Description
12	11.5	Ongoing	**Validate and remediate any file integrity monitoring (FIM) findings –** The POS Application Team will respond to any FIM alerts, as needed.	Retail, IT Director	File Integrity Monitoring alerts will be reviewed by the [Entity] Information Security Team. The Information Security Team, or the Incident Response Team, will alert the Retail, [Entity] Director of detected suspicious activity, applicable to the POS environment and Retail, [Entity] Director's responsibilities. This activity is derived from alerts generated from monitoring tools (e.g. FIM, vulnerability scanning) and other security monitoring processes to detect suspicious activity, open vulnerabilities, unauthorised access, etc. For activity deemed a potential critical incident, as defined by the Incident Response Standard, the Retail, [Entity] Director will need to acknowledge and begin to investigate the incident within 4 hours. For all other activity, the Retail, [Entity] Director will need to acknowledge and begin to investigate the incident within 24 hours.

#	PCI Control #	Frequency	Action	Owner	Description
13	11.2	Quarterly	**Validate and remediate vulnerability scanning findings** – The POS Application Team will remediate, investigate and address internal and external vulnerability scanning findings before the next scheduled scan, as needed	Retail, IT Director	The [Entity] Information Security Team will conduct internal vulnerability scans quarterly while a third party accredited vendor, Accuvant, will perform separate external vulnerability scans quarterly. Any findings requiring action will be shared with the POS team; the Retail, [Entity] Director will address the findings or support remediation activity, through scheduling and testing, before the next quarterly vulnerability scan. Critical internal findings (CVSS 2.0 score of 7.0 or higher) and above-medium external findings (CVVS 2.0 score of 4.0 or higher) from the vulnerability scans will need to be remediated.

CHAPTER 10: PCI DSS AND ISO27001

The Payment Card Industry Data Security Standard (PCI DSS) isn't dramatically different to the requirements of the Best Practice Security Standard – ISO27001, except that PCI doesn't mention any of the prerequisites required for a management framework, e.g. management commitment and ongoing improvement plans, whereas ISO27001 leaves alone a lot of the detail around how controls are actually implemented. So, therefore, one could be forgiven for believing that MasterCard and Visa assumed PCI would be additional security requirements to sit on top of an already established information security management system (ISMS).

There is no getting away from the fact that this is good news for industry as a whole. Any new baseline security standard that helps measure the security of systems is good news. For example, making sure that firewalls are only passing traffic on accepted and approved ports, ensuring that servers are running only those services that really need to be live and validating that databases aren't configured with vendor supplied defaults.

The problem is, like with any baseline standard, that it is only as good as the implementation and herein lays a dilemma. ISO27001 has deliberately moved away from specifying or dictating too many detailed controls (133 in ISO27001, but over 200 in PCI), as it did not want it to become a simple tick box exercise. ISO27001 stipulates that an entity should ensure any control to be implemented should reflect the level of risk (or vulnerability), that could cause unnecessary pain should it not be addressed.

PCI does necessitate conducting a formal risk assessment (see section 12.1.2), but how flexible would a certified third-party auditor be during the audits? Would he/she agree with the entity that the risks acceptable to one entity were deemed unacceptable to another (depending upon the risk appetite of the entities)?

PCI and ISO27001 – the comparisons

In contrast to the PCI framework, the ISO27001 Standard is more flexible in terms of scope, controls, compliance and enforcement. As an internationally recognised best practice standard, ISO27001 is designed to apply to a wide variety of entities across numerous industries. It is regarded as the de facto information security standard by many entities where information security is a strict requirement; although compliance is voluntary. Many entities that choose to certify to the Standard often do so for purposes of due diligence or partner confidence.

When properly applied, ISO27001 is based around a flow of information, which makes up what the Standard defines as a system or business process. The entity defines the systems to be certified and sets up an information security management system (ISMS) around the relevant area of business, which is then defined as the scope. Subsequently, the entity fully documents the scope, creates a detailed asset inventory and performs a formal risk assessment on those assets. The results of the risk assessment lead the entity to the control clauses of the Standard and they choose those that best address the risks to the environment. The selected controls are then documented in its statement of applicability (SOA) and mapped back to the risk assessment.

PCI DSS requirements or controls are mandatory – if an entity wants to comply with PCI DSS, then it must comply with every requirement laid out in the Standard. In contrast, ISO27001 controls are suggested controls, and each entity has the flexibility to decide which controls it wants to implement dependent upon the risk appetite of the entity.

Compared to ISO27001 requirements, PCI DSS controls are much more specific. This granularity should, in theory, make auditing of PCI DSS easier than ISO27001, but, conversely, the specific controls required for PCI DSS remove a certain amount of flexibility and could make compliance more difficult to achieve.

Figure 15 – PCI and ISO27001 characteristic table

Characteristic	PCI DSS	ISO27001
Implementation of controls	Mandatory	Based on risk assessment
Degree of granularity	High	Low
Degree of flexibility	Low	High
Management of systems	Low contribution	Considerable contribution

Analysis of the two standards shows that there are gaps between PCI DSS and ISO27001, but these gaps do not mean that an ISO27001 information security programme is unable to meet PCI DSS requirements or vice versa. What they do show is that whilst ISO27001 may have a similar type of control on the PCI-related system, the control is unlikely to have the granularity required by PCI DSS. Detailed planning when considering ISO27001 certification could allow an entity to meet both standards with a single implementation effort.

The two standards have very different compliance requirements. Generally, ISO27001 provides guidance to an entity in implementing and managing an information security programme and management system, whereas PCI DSS focuses on specific components of the implementation and status of 'applicable' controls, apart from what is regarded as 'compensating controls' i.e. existing controls can be used, providing there is risk justification.

Most entities which have implemented an ISO27001 information security management system do not have to invite external third parties to validate that they are operating within the realms of a compliant ISMS. However, anyone claiming to be compliant to ISO27001 now has to address all the requirements of the clauses 4-8 found in ISO27001, which define the information security management system i.e. risk assessment and methodology, audit schedule, effective measurements and SOA.

This effectively means that ISO27001 is now more focused on implementing controls based on risk, and ensuring that monitoring and improving the risks facing the business are improved, as opposed to simply stipulating which of these were 'not applicable' under the old Standard BS7799, or ISO17799/ISO27002. Therefore, irrespective of whether they are claiming to be compliant or certificated to ISO27001 (ISO17799/ISO27002) this is now a mandatory requirement; and therefore aligns itself more to PCI DSS.

In addition, whilst ISO27001 is more focused on control objectives, PCI DSS has a blend of control objectives and controls specific to the Standard. However, most PCI DSS requirements are covered by ISO27001 – only lacking specific implementation details in certain areas. Using ISO27001 as a means to meet compliance targets could be regarded as an appropriate methodology to meet requirements of the PCI framework. However, in order to attain PCI DSS compliance an entity's ISMS must address the specific granular requirements and follow the PCI requirements exactly.

Once again, ISO27001 (A.15.3.1) overlaps with the well-defined audit regime for PCI DSS, with ISO27001 'Control A.15.2.2 – Technical compliance checking' specifically requiring annual penetration tests to be conducted. In contrast to PCI DSS, additional mandatory requirements within ISO27001 'Compliance Section' (A.15) also require entities to ensure ongoing compliance with appropriate legislative, regulative and contractual requirements. This effectively means that two security standards complement each other when it comes to audit and compliance.

Figure 16 – High level PCI to ISO27001 mapping table

PCI DSS	ISO27001 relationship										
	A.5	A.6	A.7	A.8	A.9	A.10	A.11	A.12	A.13	A.14	A.15
1: Install and maintain a firewall configuration to protect cardholder data		√				√	√				√
2: Do not use vendor-supplied defaults for system passwords and other security parameters							√	√			
3: Protect stored cardholder data						√	√	√			√
4: Encrypt transmission of cardholder data across open, public networks								√			
5: Use and regularly update anti-virus software						√	√				

	1	2	3	4	5	6	7	8	9	10	11
6: Develop and maintain secure systems and applications						√	√	√			√
7: Restrict access to cardholder data by business need-to-know							√				
8: Assign a unique ID to each person with computer access							√				
9: Restrict physical access to cardholder data			√		√	√	√				
10: Track and monitor all access to network resources and cardholder data						√					√
11: Regularly test security systems and processes						√	√	√			√
12: Maintain a policy that addresses information security	√	√	√	√		√	√	√	√	√	

From this simple illustration you can see that most of the PCI controls focus around the three ISO27001 sections (A.10, A.11 and A.12), which address the technical elements of data security: A.10 – Communications and operations management, dealing with all aspect of change control, anti- virus, back-up and monitoring; A.11 – Access control, dealing with all aspects of user ID management, network access, operating systems and remote working; and finally A.12 – Information systems acquisition, development and maintenance, dealing with all aspects of technical design specifications, input/output data validation, patch Management, cryptography and application development generally.

This however, confirms the view that less focus is given to 'management aspects' or, put another way, less time is spent on ensuring the ongoing improvement and management elements of a ISO27001 compliant ISMS (as you might expect) are required.

If a properly developed and implemented ISMS is in place; with full documentation and working processes, it can result in a comprehensive security management approach and will give visibility to the fact that the controls are in place and are being managed and measured. Provided the ISO27001 methodology is implemented correctly (clause sections) with the emphasis on specific details pertinent to both standards, this approach should meet all the relevant regulatory and legal requirements and prepare any entity for future compliance and regulatory challenges.

Whilst these important technical sections are dealt with more than adequately within PCI DSS, the 'mandatory' requirements of ISO27001 ISMS, namely the clause sections and A.5 – Security policy, A6 – Security entity (third parties), A13 – Security incident management/Crisis management, A14 – Business continuity and disaster recovery (BS25999) and A.15 – Audit and compliance are only referred to briefly within PCI DSS. However, at the same time, this does once again demonstrate the close relationship between the two Standards and, therefore, enforces the message that ISO27001 can help an entity achieve and manage a PCI DSS environment and vice versa but also underlines the original point that it appears that PCI DSS was designed to simply fit onto an existing ISO27001 based ISMS. In conclusion, PCI DSS is a great technical standard, but still needs an information security management system to manage, monitor and improve it!

APPENDIX 1 – PROJECT CHECKLIST

PCI compliance – Project checklist	Tick if in place √
Step 1 – Project initiation	
▪ Have the objectives and sponsor been identified?	o
▪ Have the escalation/communications channels been agreed?	o
▪ Has a PID been created?	o
▪ Has the PID been signed off?	o
▪ Is there a draft security improvement plan?	o
Step 2 – Scope review	
▪ Has the scope been determined?	o
▪ Has a scope workshop been organised?	o
▪ Has the scope been documented?	o
▪ Has the scope been signed off?	o

Step 3 – Review the IS policy		
	▪ Has the IS policy been reviewed?	O
	▪ Has the set of supporting policies been reviewed?	O
	▪ Have any gaps been identified?	O
	▪ Have formal recommendations been made?	O
	▪ Has the SIP been populated?	O
Step 4 – Gap analysis		
	▪ Have questions been prepared for GA scope?	O
	▪ Have interviews for GA been arranged?	O
	▪ Have the GA workshops been arranged?	O
	▪ Have the findings been documented?	O
	▪ Has a report template been prepared?	O
	▪ Has the GA report been drafted?	O
	▪ Has the SIP been populated and updated?	O
	▪ Have the findings been presented to the key stakeholders?	O

Appendix 1: Project Checklist

Step 5 – Risk analysis		
	▪ Has the RA scoping meeting been held?	o
	▪ Has the desktop study been conducted?	o
	▪ Has the risk workshop been held?	o
	▪ Has a risk register been prepared?	o
	▪ Has the risk management report been prepared?	o
	▪ Has the risk management report been presented?	o
	▪ Has the SIP been updated?	o
Step 6 – Establish the baseline		
	▪ Have all 12 objectives outlined in the PCI Standard been addressed?	o
	▪ Has the SIP been updated?	o

Step 7 – Auditing		
	▪ Has the audit scope and schedule been defined?	o
	▪ Have the audit questionnaires been defined using PCI_audit_procedures_v2?	o
	▪ Have all seven components of the audit been conducted?	o
	▪ Have the findings been reported?	o
	▪ Have follow-up actions been designated to owners (with dates)?	o
	▪ Has the SIP been updated?	o
Step 8 – Remediation planning		
	▪ Have time lines been agreed with owners and management?	o
	▪ Has a remediation plan been devised to address any outstanding issues?	o
	▪ Has the SIP been updated?	o

Appendix 1: Project Checklist

Step 9 – Demonstrating compliance	
▪ Have the validation requirements been confirmed as being met?	O
▪ Are the ISMS foundations in place?	O
▪ Have the logging requirements been defined?	O
▪ Have the monitoring requirements been defined?	O
▪ Has a testing regime been set up (including audit)?	O
▪ Has the SIP been updated?	O
▪ Has a project handover document been prepared?	O
▪ Has the project close down been held (including lesson learned)?	O

APPENDIX 2 – PCI DSS PROJECT PLAN

Steps	Description	Duration	Start	Finish
Step 1				
	Establish PCI project	2 days	03/03/08	04/03/08
	Agree objectives and sponsor	1 day	05/03/08	05/03/08
	Agree escalation/ communication	1 day	06/03/08	06/03/08
	Create PID	2 days	07/03/08	10/03/08
	Sign off on PID	0 days	10/03/08	10/03/08
	Create draft SIP	2 days	11/03/08	12/03/08
Step 2				
	Determine the scope	1 day	13/03/08	13/03/08
	Scope workshop	1 day	14/03/08	14/03/08
	Document scope	2 days	17/03/08	18/03/08
	Sign off on scope	0 days	18/03/08	18/03/08

Appendix 2: PCI DSS Project Plan

Step 3					
		Review IS policy	2 days	19/03/08	20/03/08
		Review set of supporting policies	2 days	21/03/08	24/03/08
		Conduct policy analysis	2 days	25/03/08	26/03/08
		Make recommendations	2 days	27/03/08	28/03/08
		Populate SIP	2 days	31/03/08	01/04/08
Step 4					
		Conduct gap analysis	1 day	02/04/08	02/04/08
		Prepare questions for GA scope	1 day	03/04/08	03/04/08
		Conduct GA interviews	10 days	04/04/08	17/04/08
		Conduct GA workshops	2 days	18/04/08	21/04/08
		Prepare findings	3 days	22/04/08	24/04/08
		Document findings/ recommendations	3 days	25/04/08	29/04/08

Appendix 2: PCI DSS Project Plan

	Prepare GA report	2 days	30/04/08	01/05/08
	Populate and update SIP	1 day	02/05/08	02/05/08
	Present GA report and SIP	2 days	05/05/08	06/05/08
Step 5				
	Conduct risk analysis	1 day	07/05/08	07/05/08
	Hold RA scoping meeting	1 day	08/05/08	08/05/08
	Conduct desktop study	4 days	09/05/08	14/05/08
	Conduct risk interviews	4 days	15/05/08	20/05/08
	Conduct risk workshop analysis	1 day	21/05/08	21/05/08
	Prepare risk register	2 days	22/05/08	23/05/08
	Prepare risk management report	2 days	26/05/08	27/05/08
	Present risk management report	3 days	28/05/08	30/05/08

	Populate and update SIP	2 days	02/06/08	03/06/08
Step 6				
	Establish the baseline	2 days	04/06/08	05/06/08
	Complete tasks 1–12	60 days	06/06/08	28/08/08
	Update SIP	2 days	29/08/08	01/09/08
Step 7				
	Auditing	1 day	02/09/08	02/09/08
	Initiation of the audit (scope)	2 days	03/09/08	04/09/08
	Auditor preparation (using PCI_audit_proced ures_v2)	5 days	05/09/08	11/09/08
	Conduct the audit (all seven components)	20 days	12/09/08	09/10/08
	Report the findings	4 days	10/10/08	15/10/08
	Agree follow-up action/ and clearance of any findings	3 days	16/10/08	20/10/08

Appendix 2: PCI DSS Project Plan

	Populate and update SIP	2 days	21/10/08	22/10/08
Step 8				
	Remediation planning	3 days	23/10/08	27/10/08
	Agree time line for actions	2 days	28/10/08	29/10/08
	Define remediation project	3 days	30/10/08	03/11/08
	Populate and update SIP	2 days	04/11/08	05/11/08
Step 9				
	Maintaining and demonstrating compliance	4 days	06/11/08	11/11/08
	Confirm validation requirements are being met	5 days	12/11/08	18/11/08
	Confirm ISMS foundations	5 days	19/11/08	25/11/08
	Define logging requirements	3 days	26/11/08	28/11/08

	Define monitoring requirements	5 days	01/12/08	05/12/08
	Establish testing regime	4 days	08/12/08	11/12/08
	Establish improvement cycle	5 days	12/12/08	18/12/08
	Populate and update SIP	5 days	19/12/08	25/12/08
	Project handover	3 days	26/12/08	30/12/08
	Project close down (lesson learned)	2 days	31/12/08	01/01/09
	Total estimated days (start to finish)	220 days		

APPENDIX 3 – BIBLIOGRAPHY AND SOURCES

1. PCI DSS – *www.pcisecuritystandards.org*.

2. IT Governance Ltd – *www.itgovernance.co.uk/pci_dss.aspx*.

3. IT Governance Institute – *www.itcinstitute.com*.

4. PAS 99:2006 Specification of common management system requirements as a framework for integration.

5. EA 7/03 – Guidelines for the Accreditation of Bodies Operating Certification/Registration of Information Security Management Systems.

6. Guide 62 and IAF Guidelines.

7. ISACA – Information Systems Audit and Control Association – *www.ISACA.org*.

8. BSI Management Systems – ISO/IEC27001:2005 Information technology – Security techniques – Information security management systems – requirements.

9. ISO/IEC 17799:2005 – now ISO/IEC 27002:2005, the Code of Practice for Information Security Management.

10. ISO9001:2000 Requirements of Quality Management System.

11. Gartner – *www.Gartner.com*.

12. *www.noticebored.com*.

13. COBIT – *www.ISACA.org*.

14. COSO – *www.COSO.org*.

15. *www.csoonline.com*.
16. *www.bsi-global.com*.

APPENDIX 4 – FURTHER USEFUL INFORMATION

In the process of compiling this guide, I reviewed and investigated many different entities that could potentially help you with your PCI compliance programme. Notwithstanding the useful and imperative information you will gain from your chosen QSA and/or ASV (lists available from *www.pcisecuritystandards.org/*); it may be worth you investigating some of the products available from these entities, as they may help you in your quest to gain PCI compliance.

www.itgovernance.co.uk/pci_dss.aspx

IT Governance Ltd, the publishers of this book, also maintain a comprehensive collection of PCI DSS resources, as well as a one-stop-shop for everything to do with governance, risk management, compliance and information security. Products and services include information, advice, books, tools, training and consultancy.

www.itil.org.uk

ITIL (the IT Infrastructure Library) is essentially a series of documents that are used to aid the implementation of a lifecycle framework for IT service management. This customisable framework defines how service management is applied within an entity. It also aligned with the international Standard, ISO20000. I would personally recommend anyone who wants to ensure they understand IT and its relationship with the business would benefit from learning about ITIL.

www.fsa.gov.uk

The FSA is responsible for the regulation of the UK financial system, with the FSA register being a public record of financial services firms, individuals and other bodies which fall under its jurisdiction. The FSA has been given a wide range of rule-making, investigatory and enforcement powers in order to meet its statutory objectives.

www.sec.gov

The mission of the US Securities and Exchange Commission is to protect investors, maintain fair, orderly, and efficient markets, and facilitate capital formation. This is similar to the role of the UK's FSA and therefore some regulation ideas are discussed between these entities.

www.ftc.gov

The US Federal Trade Commission deals with issues that touch the economic life of every American. It is the only federal agency with both consumer protection and competition jurisdiction in broad sectors of the economy. The FTC pursues vigorous and effective law enforcement; advances consumers' interests by sharing its expertise with federal and state legislatures and US and international government agencies; develops policy and research tools through hearings, workshops, and conferences; and creates practical and plain-language educational programmes for consumers and businesses in a global market place with constantly changing technologies. This site has some really useful reports, well worth exploring and keeping an eye on, as much of what affects our cousins in the States usually affects us.

www.gartner.com

Gartner Research is an independent, insightful, and instantly applicable resource for tens of thousands of technology professionals on a daily basis. Despite this, it can be rather costly to download some of their excellent and useful reports, so choose carefully.

www.forrester.com

Forrester Research, Inc. is an independent technology and market research entity that provides pragmatic and forward-thinking advice to global leaders in business and technology. For more than 24 years, Forrester has been making leaders successful every day through its proprietary research, consulting, events, and peer-to-peer executive programmes. The good thing about Forrester is that it offers a money back guarantee and some of the information is available free to download.

www.fbi.gov

This site has extremely valuable and credible reports to help you. The FBI's mission is to help protect you, your communities, and your businesses from the most dangerous threats facing the USA – from international and domestic terrorists to spies on US soil ... from cyber villains to corrupt government officials ... from mobsters to violent gangs ... from child predators to serial killers. You can learn more about the FBI's work with law enforcement and intelligence partners across the country and around the globe.

www.sans.org/

SANS is the most trusted and by far the largest source for information security training, certification and research in the world. They offer renowned computer, software and network security training, certification through their GIAC affiliate, free resources for research and global incident response, in-depth training in computer security, firewall protection, hacking, intrusion Detection, CISSP CBK and much more.

www.theregister.co.uk

The Register is a useful website full of bite size IT related information; it can be used to simply supplement any information you wish to present to help you build your business case for PCI compliance.

www.nist.gov

Founded in 1901, NIST is a non-regulatory federal agency within the US Department of Commerce. NIST's mission is to promote US innovation and industrial competitiveness by advancing measurement science, standards, and technology in ways that enhance economic security and improve our quality of life.

Now for some product supporting information. Although throughout this guide I have tried to avoid the referral towards certain vendors, sometime it is inevitable. Therefore, listed below are some of the vendor and product entities that could specifically help you in your PCI deliberations.

www.itgovernance.co.uk/pci_dss.aspx

IT Governance provides a comprehensive range of information security books, tools and software, including a PCI DSS toolkit, a risk assessment tool and a full range of training and consultancy services.

www.ecora.com

Ecora's automated software solutions discover an entity's critical systems and collect configuration data – including security-related data such as credentials, permissions, access controls, and more in a centralised Configuration Management Database (CMDB). They also have a compliance tool (Auditor Pro 4.5), that appears to significantly help improve the efficiencies of your PCI compliance requirements.

www.loglogic.com

LogLogic™ provides the world's leading enterprise-class platform for collecting, storing, reporting and alerting on 100 per cent of IT log data from virtually any device, operating system or application.

www.securityinnovation.com

Security Innovation is an authority on application security and a leading independent provider of risk assessment, risk mitigation and education services to mid-size and Fortune 500 entities.

www.tripwire.com

Tripwire is the recognised leader of configuration audit and control software. Tripwire Enterprise is the first to combine configuration change auditing with configuration assessment, helping IT entities automate compliance across the data centre.

www.qualys.com

Qualys, Inc., the leading provider of on demand vulnerability management and policy compliance solutions, helps entities of all sizes discover vulnerabilities, ensure regulatory compliance and prioritise remediation according to business risk.

www.ssh.com

Founded in 1995, SSH Communications Security is a world-leading provider of enterprise security solutions and end-to-end communications security, and the original developer of the Secure Shell protocol.

www.itcinstitute.com/

The IT Compliance Institute (ITCi) strives to be a global authority on the role of technology in business governance and regulatory compliance. Through comprehensive education, research, and analysis related to emerging government statutes and affected business and technology practices, they help entities overcome the challenges posed by today's regulatory environment and find new ways to turn compliance efforts into capital opportunities.

PCI DSS available resources

In addition, the IT Governance website (*www.itgovernance.co.uk/pci_dss.aspx*) is packed full of useful information and therefore you should download everything available and digest all this free information – before embarking on the PCI compliance project.

Information available includes:

Glossary – this document defines terms used in PCI DSS v2 and the other resources available to ASVs and QSAs.
The PCI self-assessment questionnaire (SAQ)

This is an important validation tool that is primarily used by smaller merchants and service providers to demonstrate compliance to the PCI DSS. The currently posted version of the SAQ is based on the Payment Card Industry (PCI) Data Security Standard (DSS) v. January 2005, and it will be valid until the next version is released.

Payment card industry self-assessment questionnaire (pdf)

PCI DSS payment card industry self-assessment questionnaire (locked Word)

The security audit procedures document is designed for use by assessors conducting on-site reviews for merchants and service providers required to validate compliance with PCI DSS requirements. The requirements and audit procedures presented in this document are based on the PCI DSS.

PCI DSS security audit procedures (pdf)

PCI DSS security audit procedures (locked Word)

PCI security scanning procedures. The purpose and scope of the PCI DSS security Scan for merchants and service providers subject to scans to help validate compliance with the PCI DSS. ASVs also use this document to assist merchants and service providers in determining the scope of the PCI security scan.

Appendix 4: Further Useful Information

PCI DSS security scanning procedures

PCI DSS validation requirements for qualified security assessors (QSAs) v 1.2.

To be recognised as a QSA by PCI SSC, QSAs must meet or exceed the requirements described in this document and execute the QSA agreement with PCI SSC attached to this document as Appendix A.

PCI qualified security assessor (QSA) agreement sample

QSA feedback form

PCI DSS validation requirements for approved Scanning vendors (ASVs) v 1.1

Recognition as an ASV by PCI SSC requires the ASV, its employees, and its scanning solution to meet or exceed the described requirements and execute the 'PCI ASV compliance test agreement' attached as Appendix A with PCI SSC. The entities that qualify are then identified on PCI SSC's ASV list on PCI SSC's website in accordance with the agreement.

PCI ASV compliance test agreement sample ASV

Feedback form

PCI DSS technical and operational requirements for approved scanning vendors (ASVs) v 1.1

This document provides guidance and requirements applicable to ASVs in the framework of the PCI DSS and associated payment brand data protection programmes. Security scanning entities interested in providing scan services as part of the PCI programme must comply with the requirements in this document and must successfully complete the PCI security scanning vendor testing and approval process.

PCI DSS approved scanning vendors

This list is updated on a regular basis. Any ASV that carries out a scan must be on the list at the point that the scan is carried out.

APPENDIX 5 – PCI DSS MAPPING TO ISO27001

PCI Number	Description	ISO27001:2005 Reference(s)
Build and maintain secure network		
Requirement 1: Install and maintain a firewall configuration to protect data		
1.1	Are all router, switches, wireless access points, and firewall configurations secured and do they conform to documented security standards?	
1.2	If wireless technology is used, is the access to the network limited to authorised devices?	10.6.1, 10.8.1, 11.4.2, 11.4.5, 11.7.1, 11.7.2
1.3	Do changes to the firewall need authorisation and are the changes logged?	
1.4	Is a firewall used to protect the network and limit traffic to that which is required to conduct business?	11.4.5
1.5	Are egress and ingress filters installed on all border routers to prevent impersonation with spoofed IP addresses?	11.4.6

1.6	Is payment card account information stored in a database located on the internal network (not the DMZ) and protected by a firewall?	
1.7	If wireless technology is used, do perimeter firewalls exist between wireless networks and the payment card environment?	11.4.5
1.8	Does each mobile computer with direct connectivity to the Internet have a personal firewall and anti-virus software installed?	11.7.1, 11.7.2
1.9	Are Web servers located on a publicly reachable network segment separated from the internal network by a firewall (DMZ)?	10.9.3
1.10	Is the firewall configured to translate (hide) internal IP addresses, using network address translation (NAT)?	11.4.7

Requirement 2: Do not use vendor-supplied defaults for system passwords and other security parameters		
2.1	Are vendor default security settings changed on production systems before taking the system into production?	11.2.3
2.2	Are vendor default accounts and passwords disabled or changed on production systems before putting a system into production?	11.2.3
2.3	If wireless technology is used, are vendor default settings changed (i.e. WEP keys, SSID, passwords, SNMP community strings, disabling SSID broadcasts)?	11.2.3
2.4	If wireless technology is used, is Wi-Fi protected access (WPA) technology implemented for encryption and authentication when WPA-capable?	12.3.1, 12.3.2, 15.1.6
2.5	Are all production systems (servers and network components) hardened by removing all unnecessary services and protocols installed by the default configuration?	11.2.3

2.6	Are secure, encrypted communications used for remote administration of production systems and applications?	10.6.1, 11.4.2, 11.7.2
Protect Cardholder Data		
Requirement 3: Protect stored data		
3.1	Is sensitive cardholder data securely disposed of when no longer needed?	9.2.6
3.2	Is it prohibited to store the full contents of any track from the magnetic stripe (on the back of the card, in a chip, etc.) in the database, log files, or point-of-sale products?	10.7.3, 11.6.1, 15.1.4
3.3	Is it prohibited to store the card-validation code (three-digit value printed on the signature panel of a card) in the database, log files, or point-of-sale products?	
3.4	Are all but the last four digits of the account number masked when displaying cardholder data?	

3.5	Are account numbers (in databases, logs, files, back-up media, etc.) stored securely – for example, by means of encryption or truncation?	
3.6	Are account numbers sanitised before being logged in the audit log?	
Requirement 4: Encrypt transmission of cardholder data and sensitive information across public networks		
4.1	Are transmissions of sensitive cardholder data encrypted over public networks through the use of SSL or other industry acceptable methods?	10.9.2, 12.3.1, 12.3.2
4.2	If SSL is used for transmission of sensitive cardholder data, is it using version 3.0 with 128-bit encryption?	10.9.2, 12.3.1, 12.3.2
4.3	If wireless technology is used, is the communication encrypted using Wi-Fi Protected access (WPA), VPN, SSL at 128-bit, or WEP?	12.3.1, 12.3.2

4.4	If wireless technology is used, are WEP at 128-bit and additional encryption technologies in use, and are shared WEP keys rotated quarterly?	12.3.1, 12.3.2
4.5	Is encryption used in the transmission of account numbers via e-mail?	10.9.2, 12.3.1
Maintain a vulnerability management programme		
Requirement 5: Use of regularly updated anti-virus software		
5.1	Is there a virus scanner installed on all servers and on all workstations, and is the virus scanner regularly updated?	10.4.1
Requirement 6: Develop and maintain secure systems and applications		
6.1	Are development, testing, and production systems updated with the latest security-related patches released by the vendors?	12.6.1

6.2	Is the software and application development process based on an industry best practice and is information security included throughout the software development life cycle (SDLC) process?	12.1.1
6.3	If production data is used for testing and development purposes, is sensitive cardholder data sanitised before usage?	12.4.2
6.4	Are all changes to the production environment and applications formally authorised, planned, and logged before being implemented?	10.1.2, 12.5.1
6.5	Were the guidelines commonly accepted by the security community (such as Open Web Application Security Project group (*www.owasp.org*) taken into account in the development of Web applications?	12.1.1
6.6	When authenticating over the Internet, is the application designed to prevent malicious users from trying to determine existing user accounts?	11.4.2

6.7	Is sensitive cardholder data stored in cookies secured or encrypted?	10.9.3, 12.3.1
6.8	Are controls implemented on the server side to prevent SQL injection and other bypassing of entity side-input controls?	12.2.1
Implement strong access control Measures		
Requirement 7: Restrict access to data by business need-to-know		
7.1	Is access to payment card account numbers restricted for users on a need-to-know basis?	11.1.1
Requirement 8: Assign a unique ID to each person with computer access		
8.1	Are all users required to authenticate using, at a minimum, a unique username and password?	11.2.1

8.2	If employees, administrators, or third parties access the network remotely, is remote access software (such as PCAnywhere, dial-in, or VPN) configured with a unique username and password and with encryption and other security features turned on?	11.7.2
8.3	Are all passwords on network devices and systems encrypted?	11.2.3, 11.5.1, 11.5.3
8.4	When an employee leaves the entity, are that employee's user accounts and passwords immediately revoked?	8.3.3
8.5	Are all user accounts reviewed on a regular basis to ensure that malicious, out-of-date, or unknown accounts do not exist?	11.2.4
8.6	Are non-consumer accounts that are not used for a lengthy amount of time (inactive accounts) automatically disabled in the system after a pre-defined period?	11.2.1

8.7	Are accounts used by vendors for remote maintenance enabled only during the time needed?	11.4.4
8.8	Are group, shared, or generic accounts and passwords prohibited for non-consumer users?	11.2.3
8.9	Are non-consumer users required to change their passwords on a pre-defined regular basis?	11.3.1, 11.5.3
8.10	Is there a password policy for non-consumer users that enforces the use of strong passwords and prevents the resubmission of previously used passwords?	11.5.3
8.11	Is there an account-lockout mechanism that blocks a malicious user from obtaining access to an account by multiple password retries or brute force?	11.5.1

Requirement 9: Restrict physical access to cardholder data		
9.1	Are there multiple physical security controls (such as badges, escorts, or mantraps) in place that would prevent unauthorised individuals from gaining access to the facility?	9.1.2
9.2	If wireless technology is used, do you restrict access to wireless access points, wireless gateways, and wireless handheld devices?	9.1.3
9.3	Are equipment (such as servers, workstations, laptops, and hard drives) and media containing cardholder data physically protected against unauthorised access?	9.1.3
9.4	Is all cardholder data printed on paper or received by fax protected against unauthorised access?	10.8.1
9.5	Are procedures in place to handle secure distribution and disposal of back-up media and other media containing sensitive cardholder data?	10.5.1

9.6	Are all media devices that store cardholder data properly inventoried and securely stored?	7.1.1
9.7	Is cardholder data deleted or destroyed before it is physically disposed (for example, by shredding papers or degaussing back-up media)?	9.26, 10.7.2
Regularly monitor and test network		
Requirement 10: Track and monitor all access to network resources and cardholder data		
10.1	Is all access to cardholder data, including root/administration access, logged?	10.10.4, 15.3.1
10.2	Do access control logs contain successful and unsuccessful log-in attempts and access to audit logs?	11.5.1
10.3	Are all critical system clocks and times synchronised, and do logs include date and time stamp?	10.10.6, 10.10.2

10.4	Are the firewall, router, wireless access points, and authentication server logs regularly reviewed for unauthorised traffic?	10.10.2
10.5	Are audit logs regularly backed up, secured, and retained for at least three months online and one-year offline for all critical systems?	10.10.3
Requirement 11: Regularly test security systems and processes		
11.1	If wireless technology is used, is a wireless analyser periodically run to identify all wireless devices?	15.2.2
11.2	Is a vulnerability scan or penetration test performed on all Internet-facing applications and systems before they go into production?	15.2.2
11.3	Is an intrusion detection or intrusion prevention system used on the network?	10.6.2

11.4	Are security alerts from the intrusion detection or intrusion prevention system (IDS/IPS) continuously monitored, and are the latest IDS/IPS signatures installed?	
Maintain a policy that addresses information security		
Requirement 12: Maintain a policy that addresses information security		
12.1	Are information security policies, including policies for access control, application and system development, operational, network and physical security, formally documented?	5.1.1
12.2	Are information security policies and other relevant security information disseminated to all system users (including vendors, contractors, and business partners)?	5.1.1
12.3	Are information security policies reviewed at least once a year and updated as needed?	5.1.2

12.4	Have the roles and responsibilities for information security been clearly defined within the entity?	6.1.3
12.5	Is there an up-to-date information security awareness and training programme in place for all system users?	6.1.1, 6.1.2, 8.2.2
12.6	Are employees required to sign an agreement verifying they have read and understood the security policies and procedures?	8.1
12.7	Is a background investigation (such as a credit and criminal record check, within the limits of local law) performed on all employees with access to account numbers?	8.1, 8.1.2
12.8	Are all third parties with access to sensitive cardholder data contractually obligated to comply with card association security standards?	6.2.3
12.9	Is a security incident response plan formally documented and disseminated to the appropriate responsible parties?	13.1.1, 13.2.1

12.10	Are security incidents reported to the person responsible for security investigation?	13.1.1, 13.1.2
12.11	Is there an incident response team ready to be deployed in case of a cardholder data compromise?	13.2.3

ITG RESOURCES

IT Governance Ltd sources, creates and delivers products and services to meet the real-world, evolving IT governance needs of today's organisations, directors, managers and practitioners.

The ITG website (*www.itgovernance.co.uk*) is the international one-stop-shop for corporate and IT governance information, advice, guidance, books, tools, training and consultancy.

www.itgovernance.co.uk/pci_dss.aspx is the information page on our website for our PCI DSS resources.

Other Websites

Books and tools published by IT Governance Publishing (ITGP) are available from all business booksellers and are also immediately available from the following websites:

www.itgovernance.co.uk/catalog/355 provides information and online purchasing facilities for every currently available book published by ITGP.

www.itgovernance.eu is our euro-denominated website which ships from Benelux and has a growing range of books in European languages other than English.

www.itgovernanceusa.com is a US$-based website that delivers the full range of IT Governance products to North America, and ships from within the continental US.

www.itgovernanceasia.com provides a selected range of ITGP products specifically for customers in South Asia.

www.27001.com is the IT Governance Ltd. website that deals specifically with information security management, and ships from within the continental US.

Pocket Guides

For full details of the entire range of pocket guides, simply follow the links at *www.itgovernance.co.uk/publishing.aspx*.

Toolkits

ITG's unique range of toolkits includes the IT Governance Framework Toolkit, which contains all the tools and guidance that you will need in order to develop and implement an appropriate IT governance framework for your organisation. Full details can be found at *www.itgovernance.co.uk/products/519*.

For a free paper on how to use the proprietary Calder-Moir IT Governance Framework, and for a free trial version of the toolkit, see *www.itgovernance.co.uk/calder_moir.aspx*.

There is also a wide range of toolkits to simplify implementation of management systems, such as an ISO/IEC 27001 ISMS or a BS25999 BCMS, and these can all be viewed and purchased online at: *http://www.itgovernance.co.uk/catalog/1*.

Best Practice Reports

ITG's range of Best Practice Reports is now at *www.itgovernance.co.uk/best-practice-reports.aspx*. These offer you essential, pertinent, expertly researched information on a number of key issues including Web 2.0 and Green IT.

Training and Consultancy

IT Governance also offers training and consultancy services across the entire spectrum of disciplines in the information governance arena. Details of training courses can be accessed at *www.itgovernance.co.uk/training.aspx* and descriptions of our consultancy services can be found at *http://www.itgovernance.co.uk/consulting.aspx*. Why not contact us to see how we could help you and your organisation?

Newsletter

IT governance is one of the hottest topics in business today, not least because it is also the fastest moving, so what better way to keep up than by subscribing to ITG's free monthly newsletter *Sentinel*? It provides monthly updates and resources across the whole spectrum of IT governance subject matter, including risk management, information security, ITIL and IT service management, project governance, compliance and so much more. Subscribe for your free copy at: *www.itgovernance.co.uk/newsletter.aspx*.

Lightning Source UK Ltd.
Milton Keynes UK
UKOW040221030812

196992UK00005B/13/P

9 781849 281867